Open for Debate

Capital Punishment

Open for Debate

Capital Punishment

Ron Fridell

Benchmark Books

MARSHALL CAVENDISH
NEW YORK

Acknowledgments

I am grateful to my editor, Michelle Bisson, for her help in shaping and refining this book. I also owe a debt of thanks to Austin D. Sarat, William Nelson Cromwell professor of jurisprudence and political science, Amherst College, for his suggestions in improving the manuscript. Finally, I want to thank former Cook County prosecutor William J. Kunkle Jr. for the valuable time and insights on capital punishment that he so graciously volunteered.

Benchmark Books
Marshall Cavendish
99 White Plains Road
Tarrytown, NY 10591-9001

www.marshallcavendish.com
Copyright © 2004 by Marshall Cavendish Corporation
Diagrams Copyright © 2004 by Marshall Cavendish Corporation

Library of Congress Cataloging-in-Publication Data
✓ Fridell, Ron.
✓ Capital punishment / by Ron Fridell.
p. cm. — (Open for debate)
Includes bibliographical references and index.
Contents: Crimes and criminals—Trials and sentences—Executions and executioners—Support and opposition—Deterrence—Retribution—Rehabilitation—Bias—Innocence.
✓ ISBN 0-7614-1587-4
1. Capital punishment—United States. [1. Capital punishment.] I. Title II. Series.
HV8699.U5F75 2003
364.66'0973—dc21
2002156368

J 364.66
FRI

Photo research by Linda Sykes Picture Research, Inc., Hilton Head, SC

Stephen Ferry/Liaison/Getty Images: Cover, 1, 2–3, 4, 44;
Andy Clark/Reuters/Getty Images: 6; AFP/Corbis: 15;
Bob Daemmrich/The Image Works: 24; Getty Images: 36;
New York *Daily News*: 51; Corbis: 63, 74;
Hulton/Archive by Getty Images: 81, 90, 109;
Manny Ceneta/Getty Images: 94.

Printed in China

1   3   5   6   4   2

Contents

Foreword 7

1 Crimes and Criminals 10

2 Trials and Sentences 25

3 Executions and Executioners 34

4 The History of the Debate 53

5 Deterrence: What Supporters Say 60

6 Deterrence: What Opponents Say 70

7 Retribution 76

8 Rehabilitation 87

9 Bias 95

10 Innocence 107

Conclusion 123

Notes 125

Further Information 134

Bibliography 137

Index 139

DEATH PENALTY SUPPORTERS HOLD A DAWN CANDLELIGHT VIGIL OUTSIDE TERRE HAUTE PRISON ON THE MORNING OF TIMOTHY MCVEIGH'S EXECUTION. THERE WERE 168 VICTIMS OF THE BOMB MCVEIGH DETONATED ON APRIL 19, 1995, IN OKLAHOMA CITY, OKLAHOMA.

Foreword

At 7:14 A.M. on June 11, 2001, in the death chamber of the Terre Haute, Indiana, federal prison, Timothy McVeigh was put to death. Six years earlier McVeigh had detonated a massive truck bomb in Oklahoma City, Oklahoma, causing the deaths of 168 people.

From a room inside the death chamber, ten survivors and members of victims' families witnessed his execution by lethal injection. Witnesses reported that McVeigh made eye contact with each of them in turn as, through a needle inserted into his right leg, the deadly stream of drugs entered his bloodstream. He died with his eyes wide open, they said.

Outside the U.S. Federal Penitentiary in Terre Haute, three groups with distinctly different agendas had gathered.

Death penalty opponents made up one group. Some held flickering candles in holders fashioned from milk cartons. Others held signs. One sign read, "I'm sorry, Tim." One death penalty opponent, a twenty-one-year-old student, told a reporter, "The death penalty is vengeance. It's not justice."

A short distance away, death penalty supporters displayed signs of their own. One read, "Remember the victims." Another, "Thou shalt not kill and live." One death penalty supporter said, "We're here for the 168 people who died and the hundreds more who were injured. We want them to know that we're on their side and not on Timothy McVeigh's side."

The largest of the three groups, some 1,400 members of the media, observed and recorded the sights and sounds outside the prison as the execution proceeded. Afterward, they interviewed witnesses. Most witnesses supported the death penalty. Kathleen Treanor, whose four-year-old daughter had been killed in the blast, said, "I'm glad I live in a country which has made an example of this man." But Bud Welch, who also had lost a daughter, said, "To me the death penalty is vengeance, and vengeance doesn't really help anyone in the healing process."

Of all the issues before the American people, none divides them more widely and deeply than the death penalty. And none delves deeper into humanity's dark side, exposing the seemingly limitless capacity of criminals for hatred, cruelty, and depravity.

But there is a noble and righteous side to this issue as well and that is an ongoing quest to devise a system to punish the worst criminals in the most just and humane manner possible.

This book begins by examining the capital punishment system in the United States and the efforts to make it more just and humane. Then it presents the viewpoints of the supporters and opponents of capital punishment.

1
Crimes and Criminals

Capital punishment, or the death penalty, is the killing of individuals ordered by the government as punishment for certain serious crimes. Its practice, once almost universal, has gradually dwindled during the last century. Today, capital punishment has been abolished in all of Europe and most of Latin America, as well as Australia, New Zealand, and Canada. The United States remains the only Western nation in which capital punishment is still practiced.

The purpose of the capital punishment system is to indict and try defendants for capital crimes, convict the guilty and sentence them to death, allow them to appeal the death sentence in hope of getting the guilty verdict overturned or having the sentence reduced to a prison term, and, in the event that their appeals are unsuccessful, put them to death.

This process often takes a decade or more to complete and involves a great many people along the way. Prosecutors, defense attorneys, judges, juries, and witnesses all play important parts. So do governors, parole boards, families of both victims and perpetrators, reporters, pollsters, lawmakers, Supreme Court justices, human rights groups, wardens, prison guards, spiritual advisors, and executioners. U.S. Supreme Court Justice Antonin Scalia compares the system to a complex machine: "I am part of the criminal-law machinery that imposes death—which extends from the indictment, to the jury conviction, to rejection of the last appeal."

This complex machinery of people and laws has evolved over thousands of years and continues to evolve—as it must. With the passing of time, community standards inevitably change. Since laws that once were accepted as just and humane now seem unjust and inhumane, existing laws must be struck down and new laws passed, and with each new law, the system changes.

To Protect the Community

The need for a system of punishment to protect the public from crime and criminals runs all through human history. Today in the United States, capital punishment is reserved for only the most brutal of crimes and criminals—the so-called worst of the worst. In some ancient societies, though, death was the sole punishment for any crime. The Draconian Code, established in Greece in 621 B.C.E., is a classic example of a harsh legal code. The ancient Greek historian Plutarch described the code in his book *Lives*: "Under the Draconian code almost any kind of offense was liable to the death penalty, so that even those convicted of idleness were executed, and those who stole fruit or vegetables suffered the same punishment as those who committed sacrilege or murder."

A thousand years later, capital punishment was still widely used for all sorts of crimes, great and small. In fourteenth-century England, one could be executed for a crime as minor as disturbing the peace. And three centuries later, when the first colonists came to the land now known as the United States, they brought the British penal system across the ocean with them. A colonist in Virginia could be executed for crimes as trivial as stealing grapes, killing chickens, or trading with the Indians.

But the first documented execution in the new colonies was for a far more serious offense. In the Jamestown colony of Virginia in 1608, Captain George Kendall was hanged for the capital crime of treason. Among other serious capital crimes in colonial times were murder, rape, heresy—and witchcraft. In Salem, Massachusetts, in 1692, nineteen people were found guilty of witchcraft and hanged.

A common cause lay behind the executions of George Kendall and the "witches" of Salem. The death penalty was invoked to protect the entire community from a potential threat to its existence. In Kendall's case, the crime was supplying vital secrets to England's archenemy, Spain. In the case of the Salem "witches," the crime was being a carrier of extreme evil that, if left unchecked, might infect the entire community.

Today, treason is still regarded as a threat to the nation, though the execution of a spy is a rare event. Witchcraft ceased to be a capital crime in the 1700s when, in people's minds, witches turned from figures of fact to creatures of fantasy.

Fewer Kinds of Crimes

During the 1600s, more than fifty separate crimes qualified for capital punishment, but by the time of the new republic in 1776, that number had greatly diminished. Stealing chickens and horses, counterfeiting money, and other nonviolent offenses had been removed from the list of capital crimes.

The U.S. Constitution took this trend of narrowing the scope of capital punishment a step further. The Eighth Amendment expressly forbids the inflicting of "cruel and unusual punishments." The courts have interpreted this statement as a warning to use capital punishment cautiously and sparingly. In the nation's early years, the only crime for which the death penalty was mandatory was murder. It also could be imposed in some instances for rape, kidnapping, armed robbery, and treason, but never for lesser, nonviolent crimes. These violent crimes remained the only capital crimes until well into the twentieth century.

Then, in 1977, the U.S. Supreme Court eliminated the death penalty for kidnapping or rape where death does not result, leaving murder, espionage, and treason as the only remaining capital crimes. Though espionage or treason could bring the death penalty, they rarely did. One of these rare occasions was the 1953 execution of a husband and wife, Julius and Ethel Rosenberg. They were put to death in the electric chair at Sing Sing Prison, New York, for supplying secrets about the atomic bomb to the Soviet Union. The Rosenbergs' execution brought forth protests from individuals and human rights groups objecting to all capital punishment, not just for espionage but for any crime.

As the twenty-first century began, it seemed highly

unlikely that the death penalty would ever be sought for the crime of treason or espionage. Not even Robert Hanssen, who pleaded guilty to spying off and on for the Soviet Union (now the Rusian Federation), for twenty-two years, was sentenced to death. Hanssen had handed over top secret intelligence on critical U.S. government programs that led to the murders of American secret agents in Russia. In May 2002, Hanssen was sentenced to life in prison.

But in January 2003, the trial began for former intelligence analyst Brian P. Regan, who became the first espionage defendant to face the death penalty since the Rosenbergs. Regan was accused of trying to sell top secret information about U.S. spy satellites to Iraqi dictator Saddam Hussein.

Besides espionage, murder is virtually the only remaining capital crime. But while all murders were capital crimes in 1776, only first-degree murders accompanied by "aggravating factors" qualify as capital crimes today. Typical aggravating factors include murders committed in the course of another serious crime, such as kidnapping or drug dealing; murder of a police officer or firefighter in the line of duty; murder for hire; murder of a child under six; and murders committed with extreme cruelty.

The number of states that allow capital punishment also has diminished. Before the Civil War, Michigan, Rhode Island, and Wisconsin had abolished the death penalty. Currently, thirty-eight states, comprising about 85 percent of the population, still allow the death penalty, while twelve states and the District of Columbia have abolished it. The death penalty also can be imposed by the federal government and the armed forces, but the vast majority of criminals sentenced to death are charged and convicted at the state level.

Final Written Statement of Timothy McVeigh

Out of the night that covers me,
  Black as the Pit from pole to pole,
I thank whatever gods may be
  For my unconquerable soul.

In the fell clutch of circumstance
  I have not winced nor cried aloud.
Under the bludgeonings of chance
  My head is bloody, but unbowed.

Beyond this place of wrath and tears
  Looms but the Horror of the shade,
And yet the menace of the years
  Finds, and shall find, me unafraid.

It matters not how strait the gate,
  How charged with punishments the scroll,
I am the master of my fate;
  I am the captain of my soul.

June 11, 2001

TIMOTHY MCVEIGH CHOSE TO HANDWRITE THIS POEM AS HIS FINAL, DEFIANT STATEMENT TO THE WORLD. THE WORDS ARE NOT MCVEIGH'S, THOUGH. THEY BELONG TO WILLIAM ERNEST HENLEY, A NINETEENTH-CENTURY BRITISH POET WHOSE WRITINGS ARE KNOWN FOR THEIR SPIRIT OF DEFIANCE. HENLEY'S POEM, WRITTEN IN 1875, IS TITLED _INVICTUS_.

Fewer Kinds of Criminals

Just as fewer kinds of crimes qualify as capital crimes today, fewer kinds of criminals qualify for the death penalty. Mass murderers like Timothy McVeigh or serial killers like Alton Coleman have always qualified. Coleman committed a series of murders, kidnappings, rapes, and robberies in 1984. Prosecutor Michael Allen of Hamilton County, Ohio, where Coleman was convicted, said, "People like him are the reason why Ohio needs an enforceable and workable death penalty." Coleman was put to death by lethal injection in April 2002.

One of the few kinds of criminals actually added to the list of those eligible for the death penalty are terrorists. In the Antiterrorism and Effective Death Penalty Act of 1996, terrorism was made a federal crime punishable by death. The act was passed one year after Timothy McVeigh's bombing of the Alfred P. Murrah Federal Building in Oklahoma City.

Only the most extreme opponents of capital punishment object to the execution of mass murderers like McVeigh and Coleman. But who else deserves to be put to death? Where should the lines be drawn?

Insanity

For a criminal to be held legally responsible for a crime, two elements must be present: *actus reus*, the crime itself, and *mens rea*, the guilty mind. A guilty mind is a sane mind belonging to a person who is aware of the wrongfulness of his or her crime. The Comprehensive Crime Control Act of 1984 states that insanity is a fair defense against murder if "at the time of the commission of the acts constituting the offense, the defendant, as a result of a severe mental disease or defect, was unable to appreciate the nature and quality or the wrongfulness of his acts." Two years later, a landmark 1986 U.S. Supreme Court ruling, *Ford* v. *Wainwright*, held that executing the insane is unconstitutional.

But how do the courts decide whether a killer was able to understand what he was doing (*mens rea*) when he committed the act of murder (*actus reus*)? How do they decide whether to believe a plea of not guilty by reason of insanity?

The decision is a matter of judgment based on different sets of standards. Five states have abolished the insanity defense altogether. Each remaining state has its own set of standards for determining sanity, so that the same defendant could be judged sane in one state and insane in another. This lack of uniformity draws criticism from death penalty opponents and supporters alike.

Today, the insanity defense is seldom attempted, and when it is, it seldom succeeds. Jeffrey Dahmer was arrested in Milwaukee, Wisconsin, in 1991. He was found guilty of killing fifteen people, whose bodies he sawed into pieces. Police who searched his apartment found it littered with body parts, including skulls that Dahmer had carefully decorated and preserved.

Here, it appeared, was a classic case of legal insanity. If a man who could do what Dahmer did was not insane, then who was? So Dahmer's attorneys entered a plea of guilty but insane. Prosecutors, however, managed to prove that Dahmer was fully aware of his actions, deranged though they were, when he killed and cut up his victims. In February 1992, Dahmer was sentenced to fifteen life terms in prison. In November 1994, Dahmer himself was murdered by a fellow prison inmate.

"I Can't Believe I Could Do That"

John Lennon attracted worldwide fame as a member of the Beatles and, later, as an independent singer-songwriter. He also attracted a killer. On December 8, 1980, New York City police found John Lennon bleeding to death from four bullet wounds. Lennon's wife, Yoko Ono, was at the scene, trying to save his life. His killer was there, too.

Obsessed with Lennon, twenty-five-year-old Mark David Chapman had come to Lennon's apartment building with a gun in his coat pocket. Chapman had just bought a copy of J. D. Salinger's novel *The Catcher in the Rye*. On the night of his arrest, Chapman described what was going through his mind that morning.

I'm sure the large part of me is Holden Caulfield, who is the main person in the book. The small part of me must be the Devil. I went to the building. It's called the Dakota. I stayed there until he came out and [I] asked him to sign my album. At this point my big part won and I wanted to go back to my hotel, but I couldn't. . . . I took the gun from my coat pocket and fired at him. I can't believe I could do that. I just stood there clutching the book. I didn't want to run away. I don't know what happened to the gun.

Chapman's lawyers were confident that he would have been found not guilty by reason of insanity and committed to a state mental hospital. Instead, Chapman chose to avoid a trial and plead guilty to second-degree murder. He was sentenced to twenty years to life in prison.

Mental Retardation

With mental retardation come disabilities in areas of reasoning, judgment, and control of one's impulses. Can a person who is mentally retarded be held fully responsible for his or her actions? If that person commits murder, can he or she be given the death penalty?

In June 2002 the U.S. Supreme Court answered those questions in its *Atkins* v. *Virginia* decision. The Court found that execution of mentally retarded criminals violates the Constitution's Eighth Amendment ban on cruel and unusual punishments.

The vote was 6 to 3. Writing for the majority, Justice John Paul Stevens stated:

> **Those mentally retarded persons who meet the law's requirements for criminal responsibility should be tried and punished when they commit crimes. Because of their disabilities in areas of reasoning, judgment, and control of their impulses, however, they do not act with the level of moral culpability that characterizes the most serious adult criminal conduct.**

Genetic Impairment

Advances in technology may have profound effects on the way capital punishment is viewed. One intriguing advance is the mapping of the human genome, the sum total of each person's genetic information. By breaking down and reading the DNA molecules that make up a person's genome, scientists have begun locating specific genes involved in regulating certain physical and mental behaviors.

One of these behaviors is aggression. Some geneticists believe they have located one of the genes that may be one of many factors, both genetic and environmental, that help regulate brain activity associated with aggressive behavior. If they eventually find the other so-called aggression genes, their findings could have a profound influence on an argument central to capital punishment: To what extent is human behavior determined by free will (voluntary actions) and to what extent by genes (involuntary actions)?

This in turn raises another intriguing question: Could a person's behavior be so controlled by the genes that regulate his or her aggressive impulses that he or she ought not be held legally responsible for the crimes? Could a murderer then successfully plead, "It's not my fault. My genes made me do it"?

One person has already tried this defense. Stephen Mobley was convicted of the murder of John Collins, a Georgia pizza shop owner he shot in the back of the head during a robbery attempt in 1991. After a jury found Mobley guilty in 1994, it sentenced him to death.

Mobley's attorneys tried to get his death sentence reduced to life in prison by pointing out that his family tree was full of thieves and criminals, many of them violent. Mobley had inherited this genetic strain of violent behavior at birth, his attorneys insisted. He was "born to kill," genetically unable to control his violent impulses, and should not be held responsible for the murder of John Collins. Mobley's genetic variation on the insanity defense failed, and his death sentence stood.

Women

The first documented instance of a woman executed in the colonies took place in 1632. Jane Champion, a slave, was hanged in James City, Virginia, in connection with the death of her master's children.

Champion is one of the few women ever executed in

the land now known as the United States. Of the estimated 19,200 people executed since John Kendall was hanged in 1608, only 560 have been women—less than 3 percent.

On average, women are arrested for 13 percent of all murders committed in the United States. Women have gone on violent rampages resulting in multiple murders. They have murdered their children. They have murdered their husbands in cold blood. Betty Lou Beets was executed in Texas in February 2000 for killing her husband and burying him in her yard. According to the National Association for the Advancement of Colored People (NAACP), Beets was one of eight women executed in the United States between 1977 and 2001, while 741 men were executed.

Oklahoma County District Attorney Robert Macy said: "I don't recall not filing a death penalty case because [the murderer] was a woman, but there's a natural reluctance to inflict capital punishment on a woman." As of April 1, 2002, there were only fifty-four women under sentence of death out of a death row population of 3,700.

Why is there no gender equity on death row? Law school dean Victor Streib said: "[T]here is a reluctance to take the life of a woman that goes way back. When the *Titanic* sank, it was women to the lifeboats first. In the Army, men are sent to the front lines and women aren't. Women are treasured and worried about more."

Two factors—the reluctance to sentence a woman to death plus the low rate of success of the insanity defense—may help explain why, in March 2002, a jury sentenced Andrea Yates to prison instead of death. Yates methodically held each of her five children under water until they stopped breathing. She pleaded not guilty by reason of insanity. Texas prosecutor Kaylynn Williford said, "Andrea Yates knew right from wrong, and she made a choice on

June 20 [2001] to kill her children deliberately and with deception."

The Yates jury agreed with the prosecution on two of three points. Yes, Yates was guilty of killing her children and yes, she was legally sane when she did it. But the jury did not sentence her to death, as prosecutors asked. Instead, Yates received the maximum allowable prison sentence in Texas of forty years to life.

Juveniles

In 1988, in *Thompson* v. *Oklahoma*, the U.S. Supreme Court forbade the execution of offenders who were aged fifteen and younger when they committed their crimes. This ruling held for all states.

A year later, in *Stanford* v. *Kentucky*, the Court stated that "the imposition of capital punishment on an individual for a crime committed at 16 or 17 years of age does not constitute cruel and unusual punishment under the Eighth Amendment."

This ruling left it up to each state to decide whether to allow the execution of people who were sixteen or seventeen at the time of their crime. Of the thirty-eight death penalty states, twenty-two permit the execution of offenders who committed capital crimes at age seventeen. Of those twenty-two states, seventeen also allow the execution of offenders who were sixteen when they committed capital crimes.

Since 1977, the United States is the only nation known to have executed inmates who committed their crimes while under the age of eighteen. South Carolina is one of the states that allows these executions. South Carolina district attorney Wayne Bailey said: "If you do an adult crime, the jury ought to have the option to come back with the death penalty."

But there is also resistance to executing criminals who killed when they were juveniles. Napoleon Beazley is a case in point. Beazley was president of his high school senior class, but he was also a crack cocaine dealer. In 1994, when he was seventeen, Beazley killed John Luttig during a carjacking attempt. A Texas jury found Beazley guilty and sentenced him to death. Death penalty opponents from around the world lobbied for Beazley's execution to be commuted to life in prison. Only four hours before he was to die by lethal injection, in August 2001, the Texas Court of Criminal Appeals stayed the execution, but soon thereafter lifted the stay. Beazley was executed on May 28, 2002.

Death penalty opponents hoped that the Beazley case would influence the U.S. Supreme Court to reconsider abolishing the death penalty for prisoners who were juveniles when they committed their capital crimes. In October 2002, the Supreme Court voted not to reopen the question, but the vote was close: 5 to 4. One of the four dissenting justices, John Paul Stevens, wrote that using the death penalty for people who were sixteen or seventeen when they committed their crime "is a relic of the past and is inconsistent with evolving standards of decency in a civilized society."

THIS BRONZE STATUE OF THE SCALES OF JUSTICE SYMBOLIZES THE IDEAL VISION OF THE
LEGAL SYSTEM AS DISPENSING JUSTICE TO ALL IN AN OBJECTIVE AND IMPARTIAL FASHION.

2
Trials and Sentences

Taken together, the Beazley, Yates, Mobley, Dahmer, and Hanssen cases illustrate the ongoing trend toward reducing the kinds of crime categories and criminals eligible for capital punishment in the United States. These cases also illustrate a growing reluctance among Americans to implement the death penalty. This same reluctance appears when we look at the process the criminal justice system uses to indict, try, and sentence defendants for capital crimes.

The Ideal of Fairness

The capital punishment process begins with indictment, when a prosecutor decides to seek the death penalty in a particular case. The process ends, if it goes that far, with a team of executioners ending the prisoner's life.

Throughout this process, from indictment to execution, the ideal is to be objective—impartial and fair. That's why Justice, as depicted in the classic statue, is blindfolded (impartiality), and the scales she holds are balanced (fairness).

Objectivity is an elusive goal because each crime, each victim, and each perpetrator is unique. Subjective human judgment comes into play from beginning to end, starting with the prosecutor. Is this particular crime serious enough to warrant the death penalty? Is the evidence sufficient to convince a jury that the defendant should be sentenced to death? The prosecutor, usually a district attorney, is responsible for making these judgments fairly and impartially.

The Prosecution

Prosecutors are required to seek the death penalty for only the most horrible murders, the worst of the worst, so only a select few lead to death penalty trials. These are chosen as the result of a careful winnowing-out process.

How does this process work? Bob Wilson was district attorney of Dekalb County, Georgia, from 1981 to 1992. Wilson estimates that he processed 250 murders that could have been eligible for the death penalty. Of those, he chose to classify about 100 as capital cases, but the majority of these 100 never went to trial. Most were resolved by the defendant agreeing to plead guilty to a lesser charge than first-degree murder, guaranteeing him a lesser punishment than death. This left about 25 capital cases that actually went to trial, and from these, about 15—out of the original 250—resulted in death sentences.

When deciding whether a case warrants capital prosecution, prosecutors rely on a set of death-eligibility guidelines. It is up to each state, and sometimes each county, to establish them.

A case potentially eligible for capital prosecution would

Guidelines are based on four factors:

actus reus—whether there is proof beyond a reasonable doubt that the defendant directly caused the victim's death, or indirectly caused it by paying someone else to do the killing.

mens rea—whether there is proof beyond a reasonable doubt that the defendant acted consciously and purposely with intent to cause the victim's death.

aggravation—whether there is proof of the existence of at least one aggravating factor, such as multiple murders or a murder committed with extreme cruelty.

mitigation—whether there is proof of the existence of at least one mitigating factor, such as mental retardation or a personal history of childhood abuse, which might favor seeking a prison sentence instead of death. As with aggravating factors, mitigating factors vary from state to state.

get a yes answer to the first three factors and a no answer to the fourth.

After considering these four death-eligibility factors, the prosecutor must decide between seeking the death penalty or a prison sentence. Sometimes the decision hinges on a small detail. In one case, a surveillance tape caught the defendant killing a convenience store clerk during a robbery and then fleeing. Moments later, though, the killer returned to wipe the glass on the front door free of fingerprints. This final, methodical act swayed the prosecutor to seek the death penalty by helping to establish *mens rea.* "It may seem like an itty-bitty thing," he said. "[But] I thought that was significant."

The Defense

The task of the defense in a capital case is to give the accused the best possible chance of being found innocent, or, failing that, of avoiding the death penalty. Every capital defendant is entitled to a fair and impartial trial. However, money plays an important role in determining fairness and impartiality. The vast majority of people accused of violent crimes are poor. In a landmark Supreme Court case from 1963, *Gideon* v. *Wainwright*, the Court stated: "[I]n our adversary system of criminal justice, any person haled into court, who is too poor to hire a lawyer, cannot be assured a fair trial unless counsel is provided for him."

Before *Gideon*, poor defendants sometimes went to trial without legal representation, but never after. No indigent defendant in a capital case is ever unrepresented by counsel. But the quality of that counsel varies from state to state.

How important is it for a defendant facing the death penalty to have a competent lawyer experienced in capital cases? The American Bar Association has stated: "In case after case, decisions about who will die and who will not turn not on the nature of the offense the defendant is charged with committing, but rather on the nature of the legal representation the defendant receives."

Some states, including New York, New Jersey, and Illinois, spend millions of dollars each year to provide experienced teams of lawyers and investigators to defendants in death penalty trials.

Other states do not. Mississippi has no statewide public

defender system. Instead, the court appoints and pays a local attorney to represent indigent defendants. State budgets are often too low to hire competent legal counsel. In Mississippi, court-appointed attorneys are typically paid less than one-tenth of what a private attorney would charge. Capital punishment opponents point out the disparity between the quality of counsel that poor defendants receive in states such as New York compared to states such as Mississippi.

The Jury

Jury members are U.S. citizens selected by prosecutors and defense attorneys from a pool of potential jurors. For a capital case, potential jurors must be what prosecutors and defense attorneys call death-qualified. They must state that they would be willing to call for the death penalty if circumstances warranted it. Anyone who would automatically vote against a death sentence no matter what the circumstances cannot serve on a jury in a capital case, since one possible verdict is a sentence of death. Capital punishment opponents claim that allowing only death-qualified jurors results in juries that are more likely to side with the prosecution, which is a violation of the Sixth Amendment's guarantee of a public trial "by an impartial jury of the state and district wherein the crime shall have been committed."

Jury selection is vitally important to both the prosecution and the defense. Each side wants jury members it feels will reach the verdict it seeks. During the selection process, each potential juror is questioned by prosecution and defense attorneys in turn. Both sides must agree on each jury member. Each side is allotted a certain number of peremptory strikes, by which it can dismiss potential jurors without stating a reason. Beyond the allotted number, it must state a specific and legitimate reason for dismissal.

The U.S. Supreme Court has ruled that neither prosecutors nor defense attorneys may use a juror's race as reason for dismissal. This ruling was put to the test in the appeal case of Thomas Miller-El, who was found guilty of killing Thomas Walker, a hotel receptionist, during a robbery in Texas in 1985.

Miller-El, who is African American, was sentenced to death by a twelve-person jury, of whom only one person was black. Prosecutors had dismissed ten of eleven prospective African-American jurors. These dismissals, clearly based on race, had resulted in a jury prejudiced in favor of sentencing him to death, Miller-El claimed. And not just in his case. Miller-El's appeal stated that he was one of fifteen African-American men sentenced to death in Dallas County, Texas, between 1980 and 1986. And of the 180 jurors at those trials, only 5 were African American. Prosecutors had used peremptory strikes to dismiss nearly every African American qualified to serve on their juries.

In February 2002, the U.S. Supreme Court agreed to review Miller-El's appeal. Until the Court makes its decision, Miller-El remains on death row and his execution is stayed. His case is one of many that has been appealed on the basis of racial prejudice in jury selection.

The Penalty Phase

Thomas Miller-El, like other capital defendants found guilty, had what amounted to two separate trials: one to determine guilt (guilt phase) and another to decide between a death sentence and a prison sentence (penalty phase). The same jury serves in both phases. During the penalty phase, the jury considers aggravating factors, which point toward a death sentence, and mitigating factors, which point toward a prison sentence. Then the judge must follow their decision.

This was not always so. Before June 2002, judges in nine of the thirty-eight death penalty states either passed sentence themselves, without input from a jury, or had the power to overturn a jury's sentencing decision if they wished.

Death penalty opponents believed that giving judges this sentencing power was unfair. They objected to what they saw as pro-death-penalty bias on the part of some judges. Opponents attributed this bias to the fact that many judges are elected in districts in which the majority of voters favor capital punishment, so judges make campaign promises to be tough on criminals in order to get elected. Opponents cite examples of outspoken judges who have made a point of publicly broadcasting their "tough on crime" attitudes. One judge suggested that vans might be used to transport death row inmates to court. "Could we arrange for a van to blow up on the way down here?" he asked. Another judge, after signing a death warrant, decorated it with a happy face drawing.

This show of obvious bias casts serious doubt on these judges' ability to be objective in death penalty cases. No matter what their personal opinions on capital punishment, judges are pledged to be fair and impartial. In a 1966 speech to the American Bar Association, Supreme Court Justice John Paul Stevens said that "a campaign promise to be 'tough on crime' or to 'enforce the death penalty,' is evidence of bias that should disqualify a [judge] from sitting in criminal cases."

Judges finally lost their power to control sentencing in capital cases in June 2002, when the U.S. Supreme Court handed down their decision in *Ring* v. *Arizona*. The ruling hinged on the Constitution's Sixth Amendment guarantee of a trial by a jury of one's peers in the penalty phase of a capital case as well as the guilt phase. After the *Ring* decision, only juries would determine whether a guilty defendant would receive the death penalty.

The Appeals Phase

Once a death sentence is handed down, the appeals phase begins. Every death sentence is automatically reviewed at least once by a court of appeals, where a panel of appellate judges examine the transcript of the original trial. In his or her appeal, the prisoner claims that mistakes made at trial contributed unfairly to determination of the death sentence, and the sentence ought rightfully to be overturned. Appellate judges pay special attention to the mitigating and aggravating factors in determining whether the death penalty was fairly imposed.

Some death penalty cases are appealed at several levels, from state appeals courts all the way to the U.S. Supreme Court. This means delays of ten years and more between the sentence of death and the moment of execution, a fact that has led to widespread criticism of the appeals process.

The Antiterrorism and Effective Death Penalty Act of 1996 reformed the appeals process. The Act made it more difficult for death row prisoners to file appeals that federal trial courts will agree to hear, and speeded up the appeals process in general. Still, opponents say, the appeals process delays punishment and clogs up the judicial system.

However, the process is lengthy in order to be fair. Once a prisoner is executed, that execution cannot be undone. Extreme care must be taken to make sure that only prisoners who are truly guilty are actually executed, and time is part of that care. As later chapters will show, innocent prisoners have been saved from execution thanks to the appeals process.

Clemency

After a prisoner has exhausted his or her appeals and the execution date approaches, the prisoner can still be granted clemency. He can still have his death sentence commuted to life in prison in the name of mercy.

Each state has its own clemency process. Tennessee's is typical: "The defendant may petition the governor for executive clemency. The governor may grant a clemency hearing or deny the clemency petition with no hearing. If a hearing is granted, the governor's designees will issue a report which the governor may consider in making a clemency decision."

The designees are members of a committee selected by the governor to give the prisoner's case one final review, including all the aggravating and mitigating factors. This last-ditch request is rarely granted. Between 1973 and 1999, of more than 6,000 death sentences nationwide, only 40 appeals for clemency were successful.

Beyond clemency lies the final step in the capital punishment process, the end of the road, execution.

3
Executions and Executioners

Nearly everyone has a built-in aversion to taking the life of another human being, a powerful psychological resistance to participating, no matter how indirectly, in a killing, even if the victim is himself a killer. Our aversion may even intensify when the victim is as doomed and helpless as a condemned man. Russian author Ivan Turgenev witnessed the execution of a murderer in Paris in 1870. Here is his reaction: "Not one of us, absolutely no one looked like a man who realized he had been present at the performance of an act of social justice; everyone tried to turn away in spirit and, as it were, shake off the responsibility for the murder."

A host of people, from the prosecutor who sought the original capital indictment to the governor who denied the prisoner's final clemency request, are indirectly responsible for the final result. They are all part of what Justice Antonin Scalia calls "the criminal-law machinery that imposes death." But none of these people will be directly responsible for the final act of taking the prisoner's life, the execution.

No part of the capital punishment process stirs up more passion and controversy than the execution itself. Every last detail has been examined and questioned and changed over time.

Where will the condemned man spend his final twenty-four hours?

What will he be allowed to eat for his last meal?

Where and when will the execution take place?

Who will witness the event?

Who will throw the electrical switch or release the gas or inject the poison?

And the toughest question of all: How can we kill most humanely, with as little pain for the prisoner as possible?

Hanging

Humane is a relative term that changes over time. The quest for the most humane method of capital execution begins with hanging. Hanging was considered more humane than earlier methods, such as crucifixion, boiling, burning at the stake, and stoning, with torture often inflicted first. By the seventeenth century, when the first Europeans arrived in North America, hanging was the dominant form of execution.

Since then, the basic process of putting a condemned prisoner to death by hanging has changed very little. On a raised platform called the gallows, the prisoner stands with his hands bound and a hood pulled over his head. The executioner, wearing a hood with eyeholes, places the

ON AUGUST 14, 1936, IN OWENSBORO, KENTUCKY, MORE THAN 15,000 PEOPLE WITNESSED THE HANGING OF TWENTY-TWO-YEAR-OLD RAINEY BETHEA. OUTRAGE OVER THE GRUESOME SPECTACLE HELPED MAKE IT THE LAST PUBLIC EXECUTION IN THE UNITED STATES.

noose around the prisoner's neck, then releases a trap door through which the prisoner drops until the rope snaps tight.

Then, according to the 1990 state of Delaware *Execution by Hanging Operation and Instruction Manual*: "The force of this drop and stop breaks the bones in the executee's neck and severs his spinal cord causing him to go into medical shock and be rendered unconscious. At this point the executee strangles to death."

The Delaware manual calls this procedure "the only humane form of hanging." Death comes swiftly—provided the rope is the right length in relation to the prisoner's weight. If the rope is too short, though, the result may be a painful strangulation with "unconsciousness occurring between two and four minutes and death within ten. . . ." If the rope is too long, the prisoner may be decapitated.

Hanging is still authorized in only three states, Washington, Delaware, and New Hampshire, and there have been only three hangings in the United States since 1977. What was once seen as a humane alternative to more violent forms of execution now appears primitive and inhumane itself. It is doubtful that this method of execution will be used again in the United States.

The Firing Squad

Like hanging, death by firing squad has been used in modern times only rarely. As with other methods of execution, the process is staged like a ritual, with great care and solemnity, step by step. First, the prisoner is strapped into a chair surrounded by sandbags to absorb his blood. Then, a black hood is pulled over his head. A doctor uses a stethoscope to locate his heart and pins a circular white cloth target over it.

The target is for the benefit of the four or five men standing in a canvas enclosure twenty feet away. They are armed with .30-caliber rifles that they fire through a slot in the canvas. One rifle contains a blank so that no one can know for sure who actually fired the fatal bullet. If the shooters' aims are true, the prisoner dies quickly. If not, he or she slowly bleeds to death.

In 1977, convicted murderer Gary Gilmore had the option of choosing his method of execution. He chose death by firing squad. In 1996, another convicted murderer, John Albert Taylor, did the same. Both executions took place in Utah, one of only three states, including Idaho and Oklahoma, which allow it. Like hanging, death by firing squad has been replaced by increasingly more sophisticated methods of execution designed to take human life more swiftly and humanely.

The Electric Chair

William Kemmler earned a small place in history not by doing something memorable—but by having something memorable done to him. Kemmler killed his common law wife with a hatchet, but that was not what earned him his modest fame. William Kemmler was the first prisoner to be executed by electrocution. He was put to death in New York's Auburn Prison on August 6, 1890.

At the time, the public saw electricity as a powerful and miraculous technological phenomenon. Despite the gruesome end results, the public saw electrocution, with the subject seated in a chair, as a more humane method of execution than hanging, which left the subject swinging in midair.

The process has changed little since the 1890s. First, prison officials shave the prisoner's head so that it will

Edison versus Westinghouse

William Kemmler's historic execution was the culmination of an all-out war between two powerful scientists pitting their new inventions against one another. Thomas Edison, creator of the light bulb and film for the motion picture camera, was the more famous of the two. Edison's new invention was direct current (DC). With electricity in its infancy, Edison was determined to make DC the standard for electrical utilities all across the nation. Edison's archrival, George Westinghouse, had his own system, alternating current (AC), which was both cheaper to install and more efficient.

Eventually, Edison would admit that he knew from the start that AC was the better system. But with such enormous wealth at stake, he was not about to give up easily. Instead, Edison took the offensive. Both men were working on a prototype electric chair for the New York State prison system. Edison elected to purposely lose this small battle in order to win the big one. His reasoning went this way: How could the American public possibly want a system that electrocutes people operating the lights on their streets and in their living rooms? He would see to it that Westinghouse's AC became the standard for executing prisoners.

To this end, Edison gave graphic public demonstrations of the "evils" of Westinghouse's alternating current. Using a 1,000-volt Westinghouse AC generator, he electrocuted a number of small animals in his famous West Orange, New Jersey, laboratory, and hired teams of scientists to travel the state of New York doing the same. In newspaper interviews, Edison suggested that capital punishment ought to be renamed "Westinghousing."

Edison won the small battle but lost the big one. In 1889, New York State adopted Westinghouse's AC design for the first electric chair, which one year later would be used to put William Kemmler to death. But Westinghouse's alternating current system eventually won out over Edison's direct current system for use in cities and homes across America.

make better contact with copper electrodes, which are attached after an electroconductive gel is applied to keep the scalp from burning.

Then prison officials escort the prisoner into the death chamber and strap him into a wooden chair. A metal cap is placed on his head and a wet sponge attached to one leg. The sponge has been soaked in saline solution to help conduct electricity. Behind the prisoner, a set of heavy-duty wires runs from a box on the wall. Officials attach the wires to the metal cap and to electrodes attached to each of the prisoner's limbs.

The preparation ritual is now complete. The actual execution is performed by two or more officials, never just one. In some states, switches are thrown. In Tennessee, two men turn keys simultaneously. The keys are attached to a blue enamel box labeled ELECTRIC CHAIR CONTROL. Computer software randomly determines which of the two keys actually starts the 2,300 volts of current flowing. As with the firing squad with the one blank round of ammunition, the electrocution system hides the identity of the actual executioner from himself.

When the system works as designed, the prisoner receives three jolts, one after the other, and is dead within a few seconds. But the system doesn't always work as designed. Faulty cable hookups, weak current, sponges that aren't wet enough—these and other technical glitches result in sparks and flames erupting from the metal cap on the prisoner's head and his flesh smoking and burning. Sometimes extra jolts of current must be administered. It has taken as long as nineteen minutes for some prisoners to die in the electric chair.

These repeated, gruesome foul-ups have led state after state to do what Georgia did. In October 2001, the Georgia Supreme Court ruled that "death by electrocution, with its specter of excruciating pain and its certainty of cooked brains and blistered bodies, violates the prohibition against cruel and unusual punishment. . . ."

Attorney Stephen Bright, director of the Southern Center for Human Rights, argued the case in favor of banning the electric chair before the Georgia Supreme Court. "This decision ends the degrading spectacle of smoke, fire, and burning flesh that almost every other modern society in the world has abandoned," Bright said.

More than 4,400 people have been executed in America's electric chairs since William Kemmler in 1890. Few people will ever be added to that number. The Georgia ruling left Alabama and Nebraska as the last two states that still mandate the electric chair as the sole method of execution.

The Gas Chamber

The next attempt to make execution swifter and more humane was inaugurated in Nevada in 1924. The gas chamber is a tiny, airtight room. The chamber formerly used in Mississippi, which no longer conducts gas chamber executions, is typical: 4 feet square by 10 feet high, six-sided, painted gray, waist-high windows for witnesses, doctors, and executioners to watch through. The 300-pound (136-kg) oval door is rimmed with a rubber gasket coated with petroleum jelly to keep the deadly gas from escaping.

As with the electric chair, the prisoner is strapped into a chair, making him immobile. Then, from pipes beneath the floor, sulfuric acid is pumped into a basin underneath the chair. As with the electric chair, two or more executioners then turn keys or press buttons. One of these activates a switch that releases a pound of cyanide salts into the sulfuric acid bath.

The mixture produces hydrogen cyanide gas, which begins to rise beneath the chair. The seat and side skirts are steel mesh to allow the gas to rise easily, and a squirrel-cage ceiling fan sucks up air so that it will rise evenly. The gas rises in a dingy cloud that is said to smell like bitter almonds. The prisoner breathes it in and dies.

A half hour later, after exhaust fans have cleared the last of the gas from the chamber, orderlies enter, wearing gas masks and gloves. They ruffle the victim's hair and clothing to get rid of any cyanide gas that may still be trapped there. Then they carefully strip, dust, and spray the body with ammonia before handing it over to the undertaker.

When all goes as planned, the prisoner dies in about ten minutes, suffocating on the lethal air. But as with the electric chair, technical glitches sometimes have led to gruesome results. In 1983, Jimmy Lee Gray went to Mississippi's gas chamber for the 1976 murder of three-year-old Deressa Jean Scales. Rather than dying quickly, Gray became the unintended victim of forty-seven minutes of brutal torture. That's how long it took the gas, which was not as strong as it should have been, to do the job. Meanwhile, Gray remained painfully alive, foaming at the mouth and banging his head against a metal pole attached to the back of the chair.

A total of seven states still allow execution by gas. But like hanging, the firing squad, and the electric chair, the gas chamber, with its record of botched executions, is hardly ever used anymore. A single method, lethal injection, is applied in nearly all executions today. It is meant to make execution swift and humane, but it is not without problems of its own.

Lethal Injection

In 1977, Oklahoma became the first state to approve execution by lethal injection. Other states followed, but it wasn't until five years later in Texas that the first prisoner was actually put to death by lethal injection. Supporters claim that in addition to being more humane, lethal injection is also less costly than the electric chair or gas chamber. All that's needed is a gurney on which to strap the prisoner and catheters and needles to administer the chemicals, a combination of drugs known among corrections professionals as Texas Tea.

The chemicals are kept in three drip bags hung on an intravenous stand in the executioner's room, out of sight of the death chamber. The bags are connected to a tube that runs into the death chamber and feeds into a catheter. The catheter is attached to a needle inserted into a vein in the prisoner's arm.

At a signal, two or sometimes three prison officials each press a different button. Computer software randomly decides which of the buttons releases the actual drugs. Ironically, all three drugs are commonly used, separately and in small doses, to treat the sick. Used together in large doses like this, however, they become deadly. The first drug, sodium thiopental or sodium pentothal, puts the prisoner to sleep. The second, pancuronium bromide, paralyzes the lungs and diaphragm. The third, potassium chloride, stops the heart. A chaplain who has witnessed these executions calls lethal injection "as humane as any form of death you can find. Basically, they go to sleep." Another execution witness, former prosecutor William Kunkle, says, "There's no cringing, no shuddering, clenching of fists. It's very clinical, very unemotional."

Doctors never administer the deadly drugs, but some volunteer to supervise the lethal injection process. In doing so, these doctors risk violating a physician's duty never to inflict harm in the course of their practice. One medical ethicist says that these maverick doctors "set off toward a terrifying land where the white gowns of physicians are covered by the black hoods of executioners."

But these doctors insist that they have a greater duty to fulfill: easing the suffering of the condemned. Their concerns stem from the fact that many prisoners on death row are former drug addicts. After years of being injected with syringes, their veins are often so damaged that inserting the needle to administer the lethal injection becomes a difficult operation, especially when performed by inexperienced medical technicians or orderlies.

Without professional help, lethal injection executions can turn into ghastly ordeals. It took a full thirty-five minutes to successfully insert the needle into the arm of one prisoner. Two minutes after the drugs started flowing into

A ROW OF CELLS AT THE FLORENCE, COLORADO, MAXIMUM-SECURITY PENITENTIARY.

Methods of Execution in States Authorizing the Death Penalty
by State (2000)

Lethal Injection	Electrocution	Lethal Gas	Hanging	Firing Squad
Arizona[a,b]	Alabama	Arkansas,[a,b]	Delaware[a,c]	Idaho[a]
Arkansas[a,d]	Arkansas[b,d]	California[a]	New Hampshire[a,e]	Oklahoma[a,f]
California[a]	Florida[a]	Missouri[a]	Washington[a]	Utah[a]
Colorado	Georgia[a]	Wyoming[a,h]		
Connecticut	Kentucky[a,i]			
Delaware[a,c]	Nebraska			
Florida[a]	Ohio[a]			
Georgia[a,c]	Oklahoma[a,f]			
Idaho[a]	South Carolina[a]			
Illinois	Tennessee[a,j]			
Indiana	Virginia[a]			
Kansas				
Kentucky[a,i]				
Louisiana				
Maryland				
Mississippi				
Missouri[a]				
Montana				
Nevada				
New Hampshire[a,e]				
New Jersey				
New Mexico				
New York				
North Carolina				
Ohio[a]				
Oklahoma[a,f]				
Oregon				
Pennsylvania				
South Carolina[a]				
South Dakota				
Tennessee[a,j]				
Texas				
Utah[a]				
Virginia[a]				
Washington[a]				
Wyoming[a,h]				

[a] Authorizes more than one method of execution.

[b] Arizona authorizes lethal injection for persons whose capital sentence was received after November 15, 1992; for those who were sentenced before that date, the condemned prisoner may select lethal injection or lethal gas.

[c] Delaware authorizes lethal injection for those whose capital offense occurred after June 13, 1986; for those whose offense occurred before that date, the condemned prisoner may select lethal injection or hanging.

[d] Arkansas authorizes lethal injection for those whose capital offense occurred on or after July 4, 1983; for those whose offense occurred before that date, the condemned prisoner may select lethal injection or electrocution.

[e] New Hampshire authorizes hanging only if lethal injection cannot be given.

[f] Oklahoma authorizes electrocution if lethal injection is ever held unconstitutional, and firing squad if both lethal injection and electrocution are held unconstitutional.

[g] Georgia authorizes lethal injection for those whose capital offense occurred on or after May 1, 2000; those whose offense occurred before that date are subject to electrocution.

[h] Wyoming authorizes lethal gas if lethal injection is ever held unconstitutional.

[i] Kentucky authorizes lethal injection for persons whose capital sentence was received on or after March 31, 1998; for those sentenced before that date, the condemned prisoner may select lethal injection or electrocution.

[j] Tennessee authorizes lethal injection for those whose capital offense occurred after December 31, 1998; for those whose offense occurred before that date, the condemned prisoner may select lethal injection or electrocution.

Source: U.S. Department of Justice, Bureau of Justice Statistics, Capital Punishment 2000, Bulletin NCJ 190598 (Washington, DC: U.S. Department of Justice, December 2001), p. 5, Table 3.

another prisoner's arm, the needle fell out of his vein and began spraying deadly drugs around the death chamber. A third prisoner was still alive thirty minutes after the injection was administered. The leather straps that bound his arms to the gurney were tied so tightly that the flow of drugs was narrowed to an agonizing trickle.

Imperfect though it is, lethal injection has almost completely replaced all other methods. Ninety-four of the ninety-eight inmates executed in the United States in 1999 were executed by lethal injection. As of 2002, only Nebraska and Alabama, of the thirty-eight death penalty states, were not using it. In the search for a humane method for the state to take a life, lethal injection stands as the method of choice. (See chart on page 45.)

Life on Death Row

Some death penalty supporters claim that death row criminals have it too easy, that they don't suffer enough while awaiting execution. This allegation raises the question of what life is like for a death row prisoner.

Life on death row is at once very private and very public. The prisoner spends twenty-three hours a day alone in a tiny cell. The death row cells at Florida State Prison are typical, measuring 6 feet by 9 feet by 9.5 feet high. But the death row prisoner is seldom truly alone. At Dannemora Prison in New York State, video cameras watch each inmate's every move, even when he uses the toilet. In prisons without video surveillance, guards conduct an hourly headcount of inmates. Inmates leave their cells in handcuffs accompanied by a guard.

The daily routine varies from prison to prison, but what follows is typical. Meals are served at 5 A.M., 11 A.M., and 4 P.M. The prisoner eats in the cell. A shower is permitted

Last Words

In some states, prisoners are allowed to make a final statement before dying. Some prisoners are repentant and respectful.

Christina Marie Riggs, who killed her two children:
"[N]o words can express how sorry I am for taking the lives of my babies."

Connie Ray Evans, to his prison warden:
"From one Christian to another, I love you. You can bet I'm going to tell the Man how good you are."

Robert Alton Harris, looking at the father of one of his victims:
"I'm sorry."

Some are defiant and disdainful.

Lionel Herrera:
"I owe society nothing. I am an innocent man and something very wrong is taking place tonight."

Alan Bannister:
"The state of Missouri is committing as premeditated a murder as possible, far more heinous than my crime."

Some are grimly humorous.

George Appel, facing the electric chair:
"Well, gentlemen, you are about to see a baked Appel."

Jimmy Glass:
"Yeah, I think I'd rather be fishing."

And some just want to get it over with.

Jesse Bishop:
"Commute me or execute me. Don't drag it out."

Charles Walker:
"I made my peace. My reverend is here. I am ready to go."

every other day. Mail arrives daily. Inmates are allowed cigarettes and snacks, and they may have radios and black-and-white televisions in their cells. But they do not get cable TV and their cells are not air-conditioned. They may not attend religious services but they may watch them on closed-circuit TV.

Typically, prisoners receive an hour a day of exercise outside their cells, usually in an empty prison yard, where they walk or do exercises. In an interview with a reporter, Stephen LaValle, a convicted rapist and murderer, said, "I feel like a lab rat walking around in a circle."

Visits are limited to lawyers, immediate family, a few close friends, spiritual advisors, and occasional interviews with reporters. Some prisoners have lived this way for twenty years or more as they appealed their sentencing and awaited their day of execution.

A day or two before the scheduled execution, after the governor has signed the death warrant, the prisoner is taken to a special death watch cell. Here, he or she may request a last meal that does not cost more than $20. During his death watch, the prisoner is kept under close surveillance to be sure he does not attempt escape or suicide.

Public Executions

By tradition and by law, each execution must be witnessed. In colonial America, before the nineteenth century, executions were held in public places before hundreds, sometimes thousands, of witnesses. Religious and legal authorities seized the opportunity to dramatize the stark reality of what becomes of those who break the law.

First, officials would parade the condemned person slowly through the streets, often in a horse-drawn cart.

This was done to attract the townspeople. The crowd would grow as it followed the somber procession out to an open field on the edge of town, where the gallows had been set up.

There, the crowd would listen to a minister, or sometimes two or three, sermonize on the prisoner's fatal sins. The message was directed not just at the prisoner but at anyone who would dare to break the laws of man or God. It proclaimed that lawbreakers would forfeit their lives to the government and then be punished by God in the afterlife unless they repented.

To that end, the prisoner was offered one last chance to seek forgiveness and beseech others not to do as he had done, and many prisoners did just that. The crowd would listen in attentive silence as the prisoner spoke from his or her stage on the gallows. Some in the crowd would weep for the prisoner's tragic predicament, but no one would object to the hanging itself.

One spectator to the hanging of a woman in 1774 expressed sentiments typical of the time:

> **To see her when she's just condemn'd**
> **does make my heart to ache,**
> **But God I know is just and true**
> **and this just law did make.**

By the 1820s, however, lawmakers detected what they saw as a dangerous swing in public sentiment toward the plight of the prisoner. Instead of serving their original moral purpose, public executions had begun making martyrs of the condemned. In 1830, Connecticut became the first state to abolish public executions, moving them into the inner enclosure of the jail yard, where only a few carefully selected witnesses could watch. Over time, other states followed. The last public execution in the United States took place in Owensboro, Kentucky, in 1936.

Private Executions

Today, only a very few witnesses are allowed at an execution, usually from six to twelve, depending on the state. These typically include the prisoner's attorney, spiritual advisor, and a few family members. Some states also allow family members of the victims to be there.

Members of the media may also attend. Since the nineteenth century, when public executions were moved into the jail yard, reporters have served as important witnesses, recording the proceedings for the public, often in vivid detail. Writing for a Chicago newspaper in 1868, the author and humorist Mark Twain witnessed a hanging in Nevada. "I can see that stiff straight corpse hanging there yet," Twain wrote, "with its black pillow-cased head turned rigidly to one side, and the purple streaks creeping through the hands and driving the fleshy hue of life before them. Ugh!"

Reporters may use words but not pictures. Cameras have never been permitted. One reporter, however, caused a sensation in 1928 when he managed to sneak a camera into the death chamber at Sing Sing Prison in New York State. Thomas Howard of the *New York Daily News* had strapped to his ankle a miniature camera connected to a shutter release cable running up his leg into his pocket. Ruth Snyder was strapped into the electric chair, about to die for the murder of her husband, Albert. As the moment approached, Howard's hand went into his pocket. When the current began to flow, Howard raised his pants cuff and pressed the shutter release.

The next day and the day after a blurry but vivid

black-and-white photograph of the hooded Snyder nearly filled the front page of the *Daily News*. Beneath the photo was the stark, simple headline:

DEAD!

THIS NEW YORK *DAILY NEWS* PICTURE SHOWS THE ACTUAL SCENE AT SING SING PRISON WHEN THE MURDERER RUTH SNYDER WAS PUT TO DEATH IN 1928.

The public responded eagerly. The Snyder photograph boosted *Daily News* circulation by half a million. The incident was one of many struggles between prison officials who wanted to keep executions private and reporters who wanted to reveal precious details to a public eager to know.

The media struggle continues today, with television the new battleground. Death penalty opponents, including politicians, reporters, TV talk show hosts, and authors, have tried to persuade judges to allow televised broadcasts of executions in the hope that the images would arouse public opposition to the death penalty. Sister Helen Prejean, author, spiritual counselor to prisoners, and outspoken death penalty opponent whose story was portrayed in the film *Dead Man Walking*, said that "if executions were made public, the torture and violence would be unmasked, and we would be shamed into abolishing executions."

New York Times columnist Anthony Lewis saw it differently. Lewis argued that televised images of executions would only transform executions into another variety of entertainment "to be clicked on and off," and that people would "invite friends over for beer, pretzels and death."

Some inmates have tried to have their executions televised. One was Timothy McVeigh. Mike Wallace, host of *Sixty Minutes*, the CBS television news magazine, petitioned the courts to allow CBS to broadcast McVeigh's execution. But state and federal judges denied the petition. The public could get all they needed to know of McVeigh's execution without benefit of television images, they ruled.

4
The History of the Debate

For the past century, public opinion regarding capital punishment has remained sharply divided, with the balance shifting back and forth based on changing social conditions. In general, when the nation's crime rate falls, public support for the death penalty falls; when the crime rate rises, support for the death penalty rises with it. Legislation on the death penalty has reflected these up-and-down trends.

During the early twentieth century, a wave of abolitionist support swept the Midwest and West. Between 1907 and 1917, the death penalty was repealed in Arizona, Kansas, Minnesota, Missouri, North Dakota, Oregon, South Dakota, Tennessee, and Washington. But then lynchings and other forms of vigilante justice took place instead. So, by 1939, all but two of these states brought back capital punishment.

Then came two decades of serious social and economic unrest. The 1920s and 1930s saw Prohibition, with the rise of violent, gangster-run empires built on illegal liquor and prostitution, and the Great Depression, with tens of millions of people out of work. Public support for the death penalty remained strong through these high-crime decades, as did the number of executions, which reached an all-time high in 1935, when 199 people were put to death.

Support for the death penalty stayed high during the 1940s through the end of World War II in 1945. After the war, with crime rates relatively low, support began dwindling. It stayed down through most of the 1950s and into the 1960s, reaching a historic low point in 1966, the only year in which national opinion polls showed more people opposed to the death penalty—47 percent—than in favor—42 percent. Lawmakers responded to this anti-death-penalty trend. At one point, in February 1965, the legislatures of twenty different states considered bills to abolish capital punishment.

Capital Punishment Abolished

The opposition focused on the Eighth Amendment's expressed ban on "cruel and unusual punishments." In a 1910 U.S. Supreme Court decision in the case of *Weems* v. *U.S.*, the Court ruled that the definition of "cruel and unusual punishments" was subject to changing interpretations, but that capital punishment itself was not necessarily cruel. In its decision, the Court cited a previous case stating that "punishments are cruel when they involve torture or a lingering death; but the punishment of death is not cruel, within the meaning of that word as used in the Constitution. It implies there [is] something inhuman and barbarous, and something more than the mere extinguishment of life." In other words, capital punishment was not cruel and unusual when administered humanely, consistently, and fairly, with clearly defined limits on the kinds of crimes and criminals that merit capital punishment. Those were the prevailing standards.

Opponents used those prevailing standards to successfully challenge capital punishment in 1972. In its landmark decision, *Furman* v. *Georgia*, the Supreme Court ruled 5 to 4 that capital punishment as then practiced succeeded in meeting only one of the prevailing standards. Capital punishment was administered humanely, the Court ruled, but not consistently and fairly.

The five majority justices agreed that standards for administering capital punishment were defined so poorly and varied so widely state to state that the death penalty was "little more than a lottery system." There was no way of telling whether the people who got the death penalty were the ones who most deserved it. Justice Potter Stewart wrote that death sentences were "cruel and unusual in the same way that being struck by lightning is cruel and unusual."

The justices were referring in particular to states where jurors were given no specific, concrete guidance in deciding whether a convicted murderer should receive the death penalty. In Georgia, jurors were told that it was up to their own individual consciences to decide. In Florida, they were told to rely on their own "profound judgment."

The Court could find no rational basis for distinguishing "the few who die from the many who go to prison." Hence, capital punishment was administered "capriciously and arbitrarily," which made it a cruel and unusual punishment in violation of the Eighth Amendment.

Consequently, in 1972, the death penalty was abolished.

Not surprisingly, the 629 inmates on death row at the time cheered the decision. The Arkansas electric chair was unplugged and turned into a barber chair for inmates. The death chambers in New Hampshire and Idaho were turned into storage rooms for food and medical equipment.

Opponents of capital punishment cheered too. But they soon realized that the Court had closed the door on the death penalty only temporarily. The Court's decision could be overturned if state legislatures made certain changes in the law. In his minority opinion, Justice Warren Burger wrote that "legislative bodies may seek to bring their laws into compliance with the Court's ruling by providing standards for juries and judges to follow in determining the sentence in capital cases or by more narrowly defining the crimes for which the penalty is to be imposed."

After *Furman*, public opinion polls showed public support for the death penalty rising sharply, from an 8-percent margin to a 25-percent margin in only a few months. A sharp rise in crime nationwide contributed to this change in public opinion. State legislatures, whose members were elected by the public, responded. They created discretionary guidelines, sets of standards to give juries and judges a rational basis for deciding who should receive the death penalty and who should not.

State lawmakers also added a separate penalty phase to the trial. During this penalty phase, the prosecution could present evidence of all the offenses the defendant had committed (aggravating factors), and the defense could introduce evidence of all the adversity that the defendant had endured, such as mental illness or abuse suffered as a child (mitigating factors). Taking all these factors into account, the judge and jury would then choose between a death sentence and a prison sentence.

Capital Punishment Reinstated

By 1976, thirty-five states had put in place versions of discretionary guidelines in hopes of satisfying the Supreme Court's concerns. In the meantime, support for the death penalty had risen to 66 percent, the highest since the early 1950s, with only 25 percent opposed.

That same year the Supreme Court responded by handing down its decision on *Gregg* v. *Georgia*, reversing its position of four years earlier in *Furman*. Since the states now had discretionary guidelines in place the Court ruled that assigning the death penalty was no longer capricious and arbitrary, cruel and unusual, or a violation of the Eighth Amendment. Capital punishment was reinstated. A year later, in Utah, Gary Gilmore became the first prisoner to be executed in a decade when he died at the hands of a firing squad.

During the last quarter of the twentieth century, public support for capital punishment kept growing and the number of death sentences and executions kept rising. Polls showed support rising above 70 percent in the 1980s to 79 percent in 1988 to a new all-time high of 80 percent in 1994.

The Pendulum Continues to Swing

By 2001 that high of 80 percent support had fallen to 65 percent. It fell even lower—to just 52 percent—when pollsters changed the question by adding life in prison without possibility of parole as an alternative to execution. Gallup polls released in 2002 showed a slight rise in support from the 2001 figures. A May poll put support for the death penalty at 72 percent, which then fell in October to 70 percent.

In 2000, Illinois governor George Ryan declared a

People sentenced to die, 1953–2000

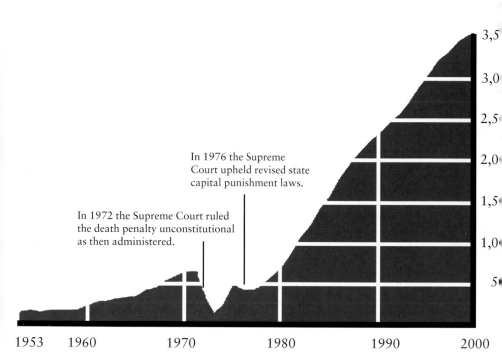

In 1976 the Supreme
Court upheld revised state
capital punishment laws.

In 1972 the Supreme Court ruled
the death penalty unconstitutional
as then administered.

1953	1960	1970	1980	1990	2000

3,5
3,0
2,5
2,0
1,5
1,0
5

Source: www.ojp.usdoj.gov/bjs/pub/pdf/cp00.pdf

moratorium on executions in his state. Two years later,
Governor Parris Glendening did the same in Maryland.
Both governors had previously supported capital punish-
ment. Executions would be halted in their states until the

People executed, 1930–2000

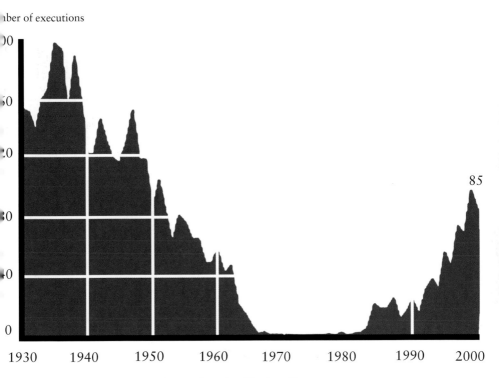

ıber of executions

Source: www.ojp.usdoj.gov/bjs/pub/pdf/cp00.pdf

death penalty system was either reformed or abolished. Meanwhile, death rows across the nation continued to fill up as more and more people were sentenced to death while a diminishing percentage were actually executed.

5
Deterrence:
What Supporters Say

The capital punishment debate that has lasted for centuries continues today. On one side are those who believe that the "worst of the worst" should be executed as swiftly and humanely as possible. On the other side are those who reject all executions, even terrorist Timothy McVeigh's, as immoral and degrading to human dignity. In between are the many millions who are not strongly committed to either side, who follow the news and listen to the public debate and try to make up their minds on perhaps the most contentious criminal justice issue in the United States.

There are strong arguments on both sides. However, supporters and opponents tend to agree on these basic points.

Punishments are necessary to deter crime and to encourage law-abiding behavior.

Those punishments must be administered by the state through due process of law rather than by individuals through vigilante action.

The punishment must fit the crime, with more serious crimes requiring more serious punishments.

But they do not agree on when, if ever, the execution of a violent criminal is necessary or justified.

Supporters believe that capital punishment is both a necessary and a just punishment for the most heinous and violent crimes.

Opponents believe that capital punishment is unnecessary and unjust, and that the most violent criminals should be sentenced to life in prison instead of death.

Disagreements run deep. Supreme Court Justice William J. Brennan spoke of how capital punishment was "troublesome to the national conscience." The death penalty arouses primal human emotions, with persuasive arguments on both sides of the issue. Reverend Jesse Jackson Sr., a crusader for abolition of the death penalty, acknowledges his own moments of uncertainty when "the violence of which individuals are capable seems overwhelming."

Jackson's comment exemplifies the ambivalence raised

by the death penalty issue. Author and political commentator George Will writes: "Capital punishment, perhaps more than any other perennial issue of public argument, teaches intellectual humility. No matter which side of the issue you are on, if you do not feel the weakness of your position and see the strengths of the other side, you fully understand neither your position nor the other side's."

Will's comment serves as a reminder that capital punishment is an issue that needs debating but that runs so deep in the hearts and minds of Americans that it may never be resolved.

Deterrence is one of the primary purposes of capital punishment. Does the possibility of being put to death effectively deter potential criminals from committing violent crimes, as death penalty supporters claim? Or is it no more effective a deterrent than a prison sentence?

The one indisputable point that death penalty supporters bring up about capital punishment and deterrence is this: once a murderer has been executed, that murderer will never kill again. Ronald Sievert, assistant district attorney in Grayson County, Texas, said: "In my own mind, it was now enough that I could deter this one defendant from criminal acts regardless of whether his death would deter others."

What else do death penalty supporters have to say about capital punishment and deterrence?

Deterrence and Fear

Supporters of the death penalty insist that it effectively deters violent crime by striking fear into the hearts and minds of potential murderers. Capital punishment has always been used to intimidate potential murderers. In 1790, minister James Dana told his New Haven, Connecticut, congregation that the purpose of capital punishment was "to strike terror into the minds of undetected criminals, youth and all persons watching." His sermon was delivered on the occasion of a public hanging, which Dana said would be "a spectacle to the world, a warning to the vicious."

Two hundred years later, John Whitley, a former prison warden, said much the same thing: "I prefer a simple hanging, on a tree or a gallows right in the middle of town, at high noon. It's a good, quick, violent death, and if you do it as soon as possible after the capital crime, the message is clear: If you do that, you'll get this."

Both men had seen violent criminals put to death and both men knew that no one wants to die. If criminals didn't fear the death penalty, say supporters, then death

GARY GRAHAM WAS SENTENCED TO DEATH FOR THE MURDER OF BOBBY LAMBERT DURING A HOLDUP IN 1981. GRAHAM'S GUILT RESTED PRIMARILY ON THE WORD OF A SINGLE EYEWITNESS, WHILE FOUR WITNESSES TESTIFIED THAT GRAHAM WAS MILES FROM THE SCENE WHEN THE CRIME OCCURRED. ON THE DAY OF HIS EXECUTION IN HUNTSVILLE, TEXAS, ON JUNE 22, 2000, BOTH PRO-DEATH AND ANTI-DEATH PENALTY PICKETERS TURNED UP IN FORCE.

row inmates would not keep appealing their sentences, sometimes for twenty years and more, to avoid execution.

Deterrence and Life Without Parole

Supporters of the death penalty say that a prison sentence, even a sentence of life without possibility of parole (LWOP), does not guarantee that a violent criminal will not kill again. Only execution can do that. A life sentence does not necessarily really mean a life sentence. As Professor Joseph M. Bessette of Claremont McKenna College in California, said, "The fact is that the overwhelming majority of so-called 'lifers' will eventually be freed from prison." Statistical studies show that if given the opportunity, some murderers will kill again.

In Massachusetts in 1984, 810 inmates serving time for murder had previous murder convictions after being let out on parole or probation. Following those previous convictions, they had killed 821 persons.

Nationally, from 1985 to 1987, 11 percent of death row prisoners had been convicted of murder before committing the murders that sent them to death row.

As of 2000, among inmates under sentence of death, about one in twelve had a prior homicide conviction.

Even if LWOP laws were strictly enforced, there is still no guarantee that those laws could not be changed in the future, resulting in the release of more murderers. Charlene Hall, vice president of Justice for All, a victims' rights advocacy group, said, "The types of people who we think will receive a life-without-parole sentence are people who should receive a death sentence and be executed. It's really a frightening notion to think what might happen to a life-without-parole person twenty or thirty years down the line."

LWOP is flawed in other important respects, supporters say. It does not guarantee that convicted murderers will not commit murders while in prison. Inmates under a sentence of LWOP have nothing further to lose by killing prison guards and other inmates.

Finally, the threat of LWOP will not deter a person who has committed one murder and has not been caught from committing others. LWOP is no more a threat to a person who has committed one murder than it is to someone who has committed a dozen. But a murderer who has killed once will think twice about killing again, knowing that multiple murders are likely to result in a death sentence.

Taking away a murderer's freedom does not take away his ability to kill again. There is only one way to guarantee that a murderer will not kill again, death penalty supporters say, and that is to take his or her life.

Then there is the cost issue. Death penalty supporters admit that it costs more to put a prisoner to death than to house that prisoner for life. Costs for housing a non-death-row inmate vary from state to state, with $25,000 per year being about average. Prisoners sentenced to life without the possibility of parole spend, on average, about forty years behind bars. So a forty-year non-death-row sentence would cost the public about $1 million.

But costs for maintaining a prisoner on death row range from around $1.5 million to $3.2 million or more, depending upon the state. This expense includes special housing for death row inmates and years of costly appeals.

Execution Update

as of October 1, 2002

Total number of executions since the 1976 reinstatement of capital punishment: 802

Year	Count	Year	Count
1977	1	1990	23
1978	0	1991	14
1979	2	1992	31
1980	0	1993	38
1981	1	1994	31
1982	2	1995	56
1983	5	1996	45
1984	21	1997	74
1985	18	1998	68
1986	18	1999	98
1987	25	2000	85
1988	11	2001	66
1989	16	2002	53

Gender of defendants executed

Female..............9 (1.12%)   Male............793 (98.88%)

Gender of victims (total number 1,217)

Female..............594 (48.81%)   Male............623 (51.19%)

Race of defendants executed

White.................454 (56.61%)
Black..................278 (34.66%)
Latino/a................52 (6.48%)
Native American...13 (1.62%)
Asian.....................5 (.62%)

Race of victims

White.................982 (80.69%)
Black..................168 (13.80%)
Latino/a................43 (3.53%)
Native American.....3 (.25%)
Asian....................21 (1.73%)

Source: www.deathpenaltyinfo.org/DeathRowUSA1.html

However, the majority of people who respond to public opinion polls still say they believe in the death penalty. So it stands to reason that they must believe the extra money is worth the extra cost of making sure that murderers do not kill again, according to death penalty supporters.

Deterrence and Enforcement

Only a small fraction of prisoners sentenced to death are actually executed in any one year. In 2000, 85 of the 3,593 people on the nation's death rows were put to death, with the number of executions falling after that. Opponents of the death penalty say this shows that the death penalty has lost its power to deter crime. If a murderer knows that the chance of actually being executed is that slim, he will not think twice about the death penalty.

Supporters of capital punishment disagree. Lack of enforcement does not mean lack of effectiveness. They insist that if the death penalty were enforced more often and more swiftly, it would become a more effective deterrent to crime. They cite the words of Supreme Court Justice Byron White. In his 1972 opinion in *Furman* v. *Georgia*, Justice White wrote that "common sense and experience tell us that seldom-enforced laws become ineffective measures for controlling human conduct and that the death penalty, unless imposed with sufficient frequency, will make little contribution to deterring those crimes for which it may be exacted."

John B. Holmes Jr., a retired Texas district attorney, makes much the same argument when he says, "If there are rules, they ought to be enforced," and that not properly enforcing the death penalty "promotes disrespect for the law." George W. Bush, when he was governor of Texas, said, "We must send a strong message that the consequences of violent criminal behavior will be swift and sure."

Criminals must see that in relation to capital crimes, punishment handed down is punishment carried out, say supporters. As the probability of executions rises, the fear of capital punishment rises. The more real the death penalty is to criminals, the more powerful a deterrent it becomes.

Proof of Deterrence

Death penalty supporters insist that there is strong evidence that capital punishment deters crime, especially when the nation as a whole is looked at during the second half of the twentieth century. Statistics from the U.S. Department of Justice show a clear correlation between crime rates and execution rates.

During the 1950s, for example, execution rates steadily fell, and as they fell, murder rates steadily rose. By 1980, just when states were again beginning to execute prisoners after the 1966 to 1976 moratorium, murder rates had reached a fifty-year high. But from 1980 on, murder rates steadily fell as execution rates steadily rose.

During the 1990s, as execution rates kept rising, murder rates kept falling, especially in death-penalty states. In 1991, Texas had the second highest murder rate in the nation. By 2002, the Texas murder rate had fallen from second to fifteenth, as Texas led the nation in number of executions carried out.

The most extensive and comprehensive study to date on the effectiveness of the death penalty as a deterrent to violent crime comes from a team of economists at Emory University in Atlanta, Georgia. The results, in a report titled "Does Capital Punishment Have a Deterrent Effect?" were released in January 2001.

The Emory study covered crimes in 3,054 U.S. counties from 1977 to 1996. The researchers used a technique known as multiple regression, in which the crime rate was expressed as a product of a number of different variable factors, including the probability of being executed for committing murder. Their report stated that "capital punishment has a strong deterrent effect. An increase in any of the three probabilities—arrest, sentencing, or execution—tends to reduce the crime rate. In particular, each execution results, on average, in 18 fewer murders—with a margin of error of plus or minus 10." The researchers also concluded that "having a death penalty law on the books does not deter criminals when the law is not applied."

Finally, there are these words from political science professor John McAdams of Marquette University in Milwaukee, Wisconsin:

> **If we execute murderers and there is in fact no deterrent effect, we have killed a bunch of murderers. If we fail to execute murderers, and doing so would in fact have deterred other murders, we have allowed the killing of a bunch of innocent victims. I would much rather risk the former. This, to me, is not a tough call.**

6
Deterrence: What Opponents Say

Death penalty opponents insist that capital punishment does not deter crime. For one thing, the kinds of people who commit murder aren't going to be intimidated by the death penalty, they say. In "Reflections of the Guillotine," an essay on capital punishment, author and philosopher Albert Camus wrote:

> **If fear of death is, indeed, a fact, another fact is that such fear, however great it may be, has never sufficed to quell human passions. . . . For capital punishment to be really intimidating, human nature would have to be different; it would have to be as stable and serene as the law itself.**

Deterrence and Fear

Camus was not referring to most people, who have developed a conscience, a moral deterrent that keeps them from committing violent crimes. Normal, reasonable people know better, death penalty opponents say. Most people do not resort to extremes of violent behavior.

When Camus wrote that human nature would have to change, he was referring to murderers, and most murderers are irrational, at least at the moment of the crime. Drugs and alcohol often help make them that way. Studies show that more than half of the people who have committed murder were under the influence of alcohol when they killed, and that two-thirds of convicted jail inmates have been actively using drugs. Intimate attachment to the victim also contributes to irrationality, creating an emotionally charged environment. About 11 percent of murder victims are killed by a loved one, often an enraged, abusive spouse.

Some murderers are so desensitized to the value of human life that it has no meaning for them. Timothy McVeigh referred to the nineteen children killed by his terrorist truck bomb as "collateral damage," as if they were enemy statistics in a battle report. Jeffrey Dahmer cut up his seventeen victims and stored their body parts in his freezer.

People like McVeigh and Dahmer do not stop to think about what might happen to them if they were to commit murder, opponents insist. They do not rationally, coolly weigh their options before pulling the trigger or wielding the knife or detonating the bomb. They are beyond the reach of the law's power to deter. To people like these, the threat of capital punishment is no threat at all.

Deterrence and Life Without Parole

The death penalty is not necessary, opponents say, if life without possibility of parole is an alternative. By incapacitating the prisoner, a sentence of life without possibility of parole does as much to deter violent crime as capital punishment.

No one should be executed. But the most violent criminals should not be allowed the freedom to commit any more violent crimes. They should be kept safely away from the rest of society, where they can do no more harm, say death penalty opponents.

Before there was a nationwide prison system in place, this incapacitation could be accomplished only by capital punishment. Now it can be accomplished by a sentence of life in prison without possibility of parole (LWOP), which is nearly universal. As of 2002, it was offered in forty-six of the fifty states, and also at the federal and military levels. While fear of punishment does not deter most potential murderers, opponents say, the actual enforcement of LWOP does prevent them from doing further harm.

In addition to isolating violent criminals, life without possibility of parole punishes them severely. It is the most severe allowable punishment short of death—and some would say it is even more severe. Stephen LaValle, on death row in New York State in 2002, kept fighting his lawyers' attempts to get his death sentence reduced to LWOP. "I'd rather be executed than spend the rest of my life in a cell," he insisted.

Why is LWOP such a severe punishment? Here are the words of Illinois judge George Bakalis as he describes what LWOP will be like for a woman found guilty of killing her three children: "It is appropriate that every day as you look at the walls, the floor, the ceiling, the bars, you will see the faces of these young children and hear these young voices asking you, 'Why, Mom? We loved you, Mom. Why did you do this to us?'" Judge Bakalis added that he would order psychiatric services for the woman "so you will always maintain the capacity to understand the horror of your crime." Death puts an end to punishment. LWOP continues the punishment for life.

As an added benefit, LWOP saves taxpayers money. It costs more to process the review and appeals of an inmate on death row than to keep him in prison for life.

Deterrence and Enforcement

Opponents say that lack of enforcement is another good reason to abolish capital punishment. The death penalty is so seldom enforced that it has lost whatever power it may once have held to deter violent crime.

Statistics tell the story. Only a small percentage of those sentenced to death in the United States are actually executed. And of those who are executed, none are put to death swiftly and surely. Of all prisoners executed between 1977 and 2000, the average waiting time between sentencing and execution was ten years.

The fundamental purpose of justice is the swift and sure implementation of the promised penalty. Waiting a decade and more to have a death sentence carried out mocks that intent.

A case in point is mass murderer John Wayne Gacy, who was sentenced to death after confessing to the murders of thirty-three victims. Gacy's guilt was never in doubt, yet the capital punishment system allowed his lawyers to submit 523 separate appeals, not one of which made a claim to Gacy's innocence. The appeals served only to delay the inevitable. It took the state of Illinois a full fourteen years to execute John Wayne Gacy. The threat of punishment if not decisively carried out loses its ability to deter.

Proof of Deterrence

There is no conclusive proof that capital punishment deters crime. William C. Bailey, a sociologist at Cleveland State University, has analyzed crime statistics, looking for evidence that capital punishment deters crime. "Neither economists nor sociologists, nor persons from any other discipline have produced credible evidence of a significant deterrent for capital punishment," he concludes.

Professor Bailey is not alone in his view.

At a weekly Justice Department briefing on January 20, 2000, U.S. Attorney General Janet Reno said, "I have inquired for most of my adult life about studies that might show the death penalty is a deterrent. And I have not seen any research that would substantiate that point."

Supreme Court Justice Thurgood Marshall, in the 1972 *Furman* v. *Georgia* decision, wrote: "In light of the massive amount of evidence before us, I see no alternative but to conclude that capital punishment cannot be justified on the basis of its deterrent effect."

TEXAS LEADS THE NATION IN THE NUMBER OF EXECUTIONS. PROTESTORS IN FRONT OF THE GOVERNOR'S MANSION ON JUNE 3, 2000, FAILED TO CHANGE THAT STATISTIC.

Common sense tells us that if capital punishment really were a significant deterrent to crime, then states with the death penalty would have a lower murder rate than states without it, opponents say. But states that carry out the most death sentences do not typically have lower murder rates. Texas, which executes more prisoners than any other state, has a rate of 6.1 murders for every 100,000 people. But Iowa, which has no death penalty, has a rate of only 1.5 murders for every 100,000 people.

Finally, opponents say, common sense also tells us that if capital punishment really were a deterrent, then a nation that abolished it would see its murder rate go up. But when other nations, such as Belgium, Denmark, the Netherlands, Sweden, and Switzerland, abolished capital punishment, murder rates did not go up.

Both common sense and studies of human nature tell us that the death penalty should be abolished in the United States, opponents say, as it has been abolished in the rest of the Western world.

7

Retribution

Revenge is the desire to get even with a wrongdoer. The need for revenge is emotional and private. It is not sanctioned or limited by law. In the Old West, when vigilante groups of ranchers lynched cattle thieves, that was revenge.

But supporters of capital punishment do not see executions as revenge. They see executions as retribution. Retribution is the desire to see persons who have broken the law punished for their actions. Retribution is a public matter, a need to have injustice at the hands of a wrongdoer publicly revealed, acknowledged, and respected. The wrongdoer receives punishment from the law, not from the victim. When terrorist Timothy McVeigh was put to death by the federal government for murdering 168 people and wounding hundreds more, that was righteous retribution, say death penalty supporters, not revenge. Death penalty opponents disagree. They believe that capital punishment amounts to state-sponsored revenge.

Public opinion polls show that Americans who support the death penalty cite retribution as the primary reason for their support. In a February 2000 Gallup Poll, 46 percent of supporters cited retribution as their primary reason for support, while only 8 percent cited deterrence.

These same polls show that Americans who oppose the death penalty believe that taking a life is morally wrong and that capital punishment should be left to God. Even in the case of Timothy McVeigh, 20 percent of people polled said they opposed McVeigh's execution on moral grounds.

Like deterrence, retribution is one of the original purposes of capital punishment. Unlike deterrence, it does not hinge on statistics. No set of numbers can be presented in support of or in opposition to retribution as a valid reason for seeking capital punishment. Retribution is strictly a moral issue, a matter of personal principles and beliefs. Here is what death penalty supporters and opponents typically have to say about issues connected with retribution.

Capital Punishment Seen as Just and Moral

A person who takes a life deserves to have his or her own life taken by the state, say death penalty supporters. Capital punishment is an ancient and time-honored principle of law and order. Virtually every society in recorded history has made it a cornerstone of criminal law.

> In the eighteenth century B.C., Babylonian law called for capital punishment: "If a builder builds a house for someone, and does not construct it properly, and the house which he built falls in and kills its owner, then that builder shall be put to death."

In the fifth century B.C., Roman law called for capital punishment: "Whoever knowingly and maliciously kills a free man must be put to death."

In the Old Testament, the Bible calls for capital punishment: "Whoever sheds the blood of man, by man shall his blood be shed." (Genesis 9:6)

This principle persists in modern times, say death penalty supporters. Here is what some government officials have said about the state's duty to enforce the death penalty.

Federal judge Alex Kozinski: "[S]ociety is entitled to take the life of those who have shown utter contempt for the lives of others."

President Ronald Reagan: "We believe that when a drug dealer kills a police officer in the line of duty, he should have to give up his life as punishment."

Texas legislator Pat Haggerty: "In Texas there is a death penalty. If people kill people, we put them to death. It's that simple."

It is not only morally right for the state to take a murderer's life, it is morally necessary. Capital punishment is necessary to help establish within society a collective sense of right versus wrong. Deadly actions must have deadly consequences. Those who do wrong must be punished, and those who commit the most serious wrongs must be punished accordingly, as long as the state, and not individuals, do the punishing. Without this established societywide sense of right and wrong, civil order cannot be maintained.

Capital Punishment Seen as Unjust and Immoral

Death penalty opponents say that it is morally wrong for anyone—including the state—to take a human life. The Bible says, "Thou shalt not kill" (Exodus 20:13). Modern religious leaders heed this biblical commandment when it comes to capital punishment. On Good Friday, 1999, the nation's fifty-five Roman Catholic bishops released a statement on the death penalty. In it they wrote of recalling "our Savior's own execution" and asked "all people of goodwill, and especially Catholics, to work to end the death penalty." And why did they make this call? "We cannot teach that killing is wrong by killing," the bishops wrote. "The death penalty offers the tragic illusion that we can defend life by taking life."

A host of legislative and judicial leaders throughout American history agree.

Benjamin Rush, signer of the Declaration of Independence: "The power over human life is the sole prerogative of Him who gave it. Human laws, therefore, rise in rebellion against this prerogative, when they transfer it to human hands."

Clarence Darrow, legendary defense lawyer from the first half of the twentieth century: "[Capital punishment] is too horrible a thing for the state to undertake. We are told: 'Oh, the killer does it; why shouldn't the state?' I would hate to live in a state I didn't think was better than a murderer."

Thurgood Marshall, U.S. Supreme Court justice, in his 1972 *Furman* v. *Georgia* opinion: "[T]he death penalty is immoral and therefore unconstitutional."

Capital Punishment Seen as Blind Revenge

Death penalty opponents see capital punishment as an act of vengeance. It is rooted in the dark desire for revenge, they insist, not the noble pursuit of justice. Supporters of capital punishment are motivated by a sense of indignation and anger.

In his 1972 *Furman* v. *Georgia* opinion, Supreme Court Justice Thurgood Marshall mentioned the Eighth Amendment as a much-needed protection against what he calls our "baser" desires for revenge when it comes to capital punishment.

> **[T]here is a demand for vengeance on the part of many persons in a community against one who is convicted of a particularly offensive act. . . . But the Eighth Amendment is our insulation from our baser selves. The "cruel and unusual" language limits the avenues through which vengeance can be channeled. Were this not so, the language would be empty and a return to the rack and other tortures would be possible in a given case.**

Laws about punishment should not spring from the desire for revenge but from measured, rational considerations, free of vengeful emotions.

THURGOOD MARSHALL WAS THE FIRST AFRICAN AMERICAN APPOINTED TO THE U.S. SUPREME COURT. IN *FURMAN* V. *GEORGIA*, THE 1972 CASE THAT PUT A TEMPORARY STOP TO EXECUTIONS, MARSHALL SIDED WITH THE MAJORITY, SAYING THAT CAPITAL PUNISHMENT COULD NOT BE JUSTIFIED AS A DETERRENT TO MURDER.

Capital Punishment Seen as a Passion for Justice

Anger and moral indignation are natural reactions to violent criminals and violent crimes, death penalty supporters insist. They do not signal a blind pursuit of revenge.

People who respond to crime with anger and moral indignation show that they recognize and care passionately about justice, supporters say. Ronald Sievert, an assistant U.S. attorney in Texas, said: "I had come from being doubtful about the death penalty to the point that as I personally approached the defendant in some of these cases, reciting what horrible acts he had done, I was filled with such outrage that I sometimes felt that if I had a weapon I might have executed him right then and there."

This passion for justice that Sievert expresses must be allowed expression. But it must not be allowed to degenerate into hate. People driven by hate are predisposed to taking the law into their own hands. It is the job of the state, through a system of laws, to keep righteous anger under control, but not to eliminate it. It is the state's responsibility to justify and satisfy that passion for justice by seeing that the wicked receive the punishment they deserve, say supporters. And the wickedest of the wicked deserve capital punishment.

In a just society, everyone gets what they deserve. By seeing the wicked properly punished, law-abiding citizens see their anger both justified and satisfied. Take away this passion for justice and we are left with a society that has grown indifferent to crime. Criminal lawyer Arthur L. Goodhart said, "Retribution in punishment is an expression of the community's disapproval of crime, and if this retribution is not given recognition then the disapproval may also disappear. A community which is too ready to forgive the wrongdoer may end by condoning the crime." And, say supporters, a society that condones crime instead of condemning it is not a just society.

Capital Punishment and the Right to Life

By sparing a killer, the state makes it plain that everyone has an equal and inalienable right to life, say death penalty opponents. Life without the possibility of parole sends society a morally clear message: Killing is wrong, period, no matter who does it, and that includes the state.

Killers should be severely punished, but not by having the state do to them that which they have been condemned for doing to their victims. Instead, killers should be kept safely locked away from society for the rest of their lives.

Death penalty supporters see the right-to-life issue another way. Once the killer has denied his victim the precious right to life, they say, the law may properly deny that right to the killer. Mike Royko, Chicago newspaper columnist, wrote:

> **It's because I have so much regard for human life that I favor capital punishment. Murder is the most terrible crime there is. Anything less than the death penalty is an insult to the victim and society. It says . . . that we don't value the victim's life enough to punish the killer fully.**

A prime characteristic of a civilized society is respect for life. By saying that a criminal is as deserving of respect as his victim, we devalue life instead of respecting it, say supporters. As New Orleans district attorney Harry Connick Sr. said, "We need the death penalty to show that life is precious."

Capital Punishment and Inhumanity

Is capital punishment inhumane? Death penalty opponents say yes. Murder, whether it is committed brutally with a gun in a back alley or antiseptically with a stream of poisons in a prison death chamber, still amounts to inflicting pain and humiliation on a fellow human being. The act of murder is still inhumane no matter how it's done or who does it. In the words of Supreme Court Justice William Brennan, capital punishment treats "members of the human race as nonhumans, as objects to be toyed with and discarded."

Death penalty supporters disagree. Rather than treating murderers inhumanely, they say, capital punishment treats them as responsible human beings, free to choose to obey the law and aware that if they don't, they will be punished accordingly. As former prosecutor William Kunkle puts it, "Society is based on free will and responsibility for your actions. End of story."

Capital punishment does not treat murderers inhumanely. It is the murderers who are inhumane, say supporters. Supreme Court Justice Antonin Scalia has pointed out that a quiet death by lethal injection is far less violent and painful than death at the hands of a brutal killer. As one Florida legislator pointed out after witnessing an execution by electrocution, the killer "died much more humanely than those she murdered."

When compared with other ways of dying, such as a prolonged death from a painful disease like cancer, capital punishment is relatively painless and dignified, say supporters. Executions are brief and solemn events with a justifiable purpose: to help preserve the moral order of society.

Capital Punishment as Vindication

Does capital punishment bring vindication and relief? Supporters say yes, that it vindicates the dead and gives surviving family members relief and closure. A woman in Texas has been waiting for more than twenty-two years for the execution of the man sentenced to death for killing her son. "I can't go on with my life," she says. "I can't close that chapter until he's put to sleep."

Juanita Wheat traveled from Wisconsin to Ohio to witness the execution of Alton Coleman, killer of her nine-year-old daughter. "I want to see something happen to him. I want to see it happen and feel it all," she said. Paulette Anderson, aunt of another of Coleman's victims, said, "It's going to calm me down. It'll help me sleep better."

It's not just the relatives of the victim who suffer when a loved one is killed, supporters point out. People close to the murderer suffer as well. Verna Gray, mother of Jimmy Lee Gray, was relieved when her son was sentenced to death. "I love him," she said. "I guess I love him; I'm not really sure. . . . I hope he finds peace of mind in the next world. He hasn't found it here."

Opponents of capital punishment disagree. They point out that execution is not what all surviving family members need or want. It is a mistake to think that relatives and close friends of murder victims necessarily want to see the killer put to death, opponents insist, not even if that killer was Timothy McVeigh. Bud Welch, whose daughter was killed by McVeigh's bomb, opposes the death penalty. He calls it vengeance and insists that it does not help heal the wounds of survivors.

Welch's sentiments are echoed by other survivors.

Among them are Dennis and Judy Shepard. Their son Matthew was beaten to death by two young men in Wyoming in 1998. It was a hate crime. Matthew Shepard was beaten to death simply because he was gay. At the men's sentencing hearing, the Shepards helped persuade the prosecutor to seek life sentences instead of death. Dennis Shepard wanted to see the killers punished, but he also believed that it was "time to begin the healing process, to show mercy to someone who refused to show any mercy." Facing one of his son's killers, Shepard said, "May you live a long life and may you thank Matthew every day for it."

In 1977 Betty Slusher's husband was killed by two men who were later caught, convicted, and sentenced to death. At first, she thought she would witness the two men's executions. Then she changed her mind. "I thought when this day came that I wouldn't be sad," she said, "that I would be happy, but I am sad. Let's face it, we're taking two men's lives."

Finally, a New Hampshire legislator whose father was murdered said, "If we let those who murder turn us to murder, it gives over more power to those who do evil. We become what we say we abhor."

8
Rehabilitation

People in colonial America regarded criminals as naturally wicked creatures who were born that way. Not everyone was a criminal, but anyone could be. Public executions served two purposes: ridding society of wrongdoers and warning one and all to control their wicked nature.

Crime as a Social Problem

This traditional view of the criminal and of punishment began changing during the 1780s, soon after the formation of the United States. People had a new attitude in the new nation, seeing themselves as capable of becoming stronger and capable of greater achievements.

This hopeful attitude, which had developed earlier in Europe, also applied to the treatment of criminals, who were seen as capable of progress. An English translation of "An Essay on Crimes and Punishments," published in 1764 by Italian criminologist Cesare Beccaria, was widely circulated in the colonies. Thomas Jefferson, Benjamin Franklin, and George Washington all read it. Beccaria's essay told them that criminals were not wicked by nature and that they, like everyone else, possessed free will. Criminals, the essay said, were free to obey the law or not, as they chose.

If crime was not the inevitable consequence of the criminal's wicked nature, as Beccaria's essay insisted, then what was its cause? Why did people possessed of free will commit crimes?

Crime, Beccaria wrote, was directed not by inner forces but by outward conditions. It was caused by social problems and could be cured with social solutions. Crime was not inevitable. It could be conquered. To this end, Beccaria called for the abolition of the capital punishment system and for the establishment of a system of penitentiaries.

Beccaria's call for criminal justice reform was echoed in the United States by Benjamin Rush, a signer of the Declaration of Independence. Rush, who would become known as the father of psychiatry, saw penitentiaries as houses of repentance, in which offenders would contemplate and cast off sin. Rush was passionate about his beliefs. "[I]t is possible to produce such a change in the moral character of man," he wrote, "as shall raise him to a resemblance of angels—nay more, to the likeness of God himself."

Crime as a Disease

Rush's call to abolish capital punishment had a basis in medicine. He saw evil as a disease, and to cure a disease, he wrote, one does not kill the patient. Instead, the criminal would be given a series of remedies to cure the ailment.

The first penitentiary created as an alternative to capital punishment was established in 1790 in Philadelphia, Pennsylvania. Others soon followed. By today's standards, the remedies were harsh. The prisoner entered knowing he would not be returned to society until the completion of his rehabilitation. This would be accomplished through a strict daily routine involving prayer, work, and physical torture, all performed in strict isolation and absolute, unending silence.

Fifty years later, the British novelist Charles Dickens visited one of these penitentiaries during a visit to the United States. By this time, it was all too clear that Rush's positive vision of the penitentiary would never become a reality. While the directors seemed to have good intentions, Dickens wrote, the prisoners were in misery:

Over the head and face of every prisoner who comes into this melancholy house, a black hood is drawn; and in this dark shroud, an emblem of the curtain dropped between him and the living world, he is led to the cell from which he never again comes forth, until his whole term of imprisonment has expired.

While the penitentiary never became a hospital for curing its prisoner-patients of the disease of crime, Rush's and Beccaria's vision of crime as a disease persisted. In 1848, an Iowa Supreme Court justice said, "Crime indicates a diseased mind in the same manner that sickness and pain do a diseased body. And as in the one case we provide hospitals for the treatment of severe and contagious diseases, so in the other, prisons and asylums should be provided for similar reasons."

Opponents on Rehabilitation

Today, few people, whether they oppose or support capital punishment, still see crime as a disease that can be treated by time spent in prison. But death penalty opponents argue that life in prison can do some good. They claim that it gives the murderer an opportunity to become a better person. Opponents insist that even the worst of the worst can get better, and that the prison lives of Nathan Leopold and Caryl Chessman attest to this fact.

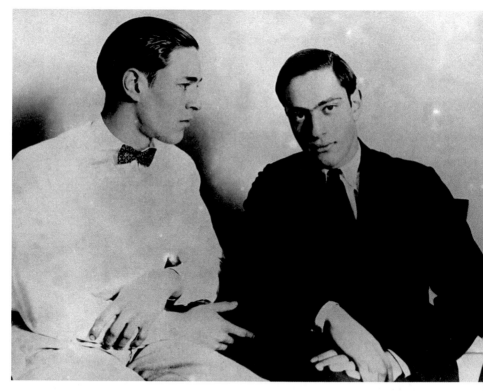

IN MAY 1924, RICHARD LOEB AND NATHAN LEOPOLD, BOTH NINETEEN, MURDERED FOURTEEN-YEAR-OLD BOBBY FRANKS IN CHICAGO. FOUR MONTHS LATER, AFTER PLEADING GUILTY ON THE ADVICE OF THEIR LAWYER, DEATH PENALTY OPPONENT CLARENCE DARROW, THEY WERE SENTENCED TO LIFE IN PRISON.

Nathan Leopold, who committed murder in 1924, was sentenced to life in prison. Yet he went on to dedicate himself to the education of other prisoners. He also did research that contributed to a better understanding of the people who commit crimes. If Nathan Leopold had been executed instead of sentenced to life in prison, these contributions would have been lost forever.

Caryl Chessman was sentenced to death in 1948 for kidnapping. For the next twelve years he filed appeals to keep himself alive. On four different occasions he presented his case before the U.S. Supreme Court. During that time Chessman also wrote four books. One, *Cell 2455 Death Row*, became a bestseller. His writings are eloquent testimonies to the power of an individual determined to rehabilitate himself while in prison.

The long years lived in this crucible called Death Row have carried me beyond bitterness, beyond hate, beyond savage animal violence. Death Row has compelled me to study as I have never studied before, to accept disciplines I never would have accepted otherwise and to gain a penetrating insight into all phases of this problem of crime that I am determined to translate into worthwhile contributions toward ultimate solution of that problem.

In 1960, Chessman's appeals ran out. On the day Caryl Chessman was executed in California's gas chamber, the governor received a thick document asking for commutation of Chessman's death sentence. It was a petition containing two million signatures from around the world. Essayist and political commentator Elizabeth Hardwick summed up Chessman's achievements: "With extraordinary energy, Chessman made, on the very edge of extinction, one of those startling efforts of personal rehabilitation, salvation of the self."

Death penalty opponents point to Leopold and Chessman as examples of the worst of the worst, prisoners who committed terrible crimes and yet went on to rehabilitate themselves in prison.

Supporters on Rehabilitation

The "worst of the worst" neither deserve nor benefit from a sentence of life in prison, supporters insist. Can prisoners rehabilitate themselves? Supporters cite Jack Henry Abbott as an example of a killer who supposedly rehabilitated himself.

Abbott was in jail for armed robbery when he stabbed another inmate to death. Instead of a death sentence, Abbott received a prison term. While in prison for the killing, he wrote letters to well-known and highly respected author Norman Mailer. When Abbott's letters were collected into a book in 1981, it became a best-seller, widely praised for the author's ability to articulate the rage and anger that made him violent. Abbott's literary fame and the support of Mailer helped him get out of prison on parole.

The best-selling author, murderer, and ex-convict was an instant celebrity. He was interviewed on national television. He was an honored guest at parties in New York City attended by rich and famous people. Then, six weeks after being paroled, Abbott killed again, stabbing a man to death outside a New York City restaurant. He was returned to prison, where he remained until February 2002, when he was found hanging in his prison cell. Jack Henry Abbott had been his own executioner.

Not long after the first U.S. penitentiary was established in 1790, hopes for reforming prisoners began to fade. People soon came to accept the fact that penitentiaries would always be places for punishment, not rehabilitation. Author and history professor Garry Wills describes the effects of modern prison life this way:

> **Prisons teach crime, instill it, inure men to it, trap men in it as a way of life. How could they do otherwise? The criminal is sequestered with other criminals, in conditions exacerbating the lowest drives of lonely and stranded men, men deprived of loved ones, of dignifying work, of pacifying amenities.**

To expect a person to change for the better in a prison environment is an unrealistic expectation—and an inappropriate one. It is not the duty of the legal system to "cure" prisoners, death penalty supporters say. Criminals are being punished for committing willful acts, not for being burdened with a crippling illness. The victim deserves our compassion, not the criminal. The "worst of the worst" must be seen for what they are, willful murderers, and must be given what they deserve, the death penalty.

HOWARD UNIVERSITY STUDENT MARPESSA ANDREWS, ALONG WITH FELLOW AMNESTY INTERNATIONAL ACTIVISTS, PROTESTS CAPITAL PUNISHMENT AT THE U.S. JUSTICE DEPARTMENT BUILDING IN WASHINGTON, D.C.

9
Bias

The ideal of blind justice means an absence of bias. Ideally, a criminal's punishment is in no way influenced by the race of the criminal or victim, the economic status of the criminal, or the state or county in which the crime was committed.

But death penalty opponents argue that race, economic status, and geography exert a powerful influence on who gets the death penalty and who does not. And, they argue, in light of this bias, the death penalty system should be either radically reformed or abolished.

The Race Factor

Before the Civil War, one punishment for a slave committing a crime against his master, such as running away, was lynching. Runaway slaves were sometimes lynched as an example to other slaves. The captured runaway was hanged by his accusers without a trial, and the people who did the hanging could do so without fear of being punished themselves.

After the abolition of slavery, the underlying prejudicial attitudes of whites toward blacks persisted, and so did the illegal practice of lynching. Between 1880 and 1920, an estimated 3,000 people were lynched. Nearly all the victims were African Americans killed by white mobs in southern states.

Prejudice against African Americans carried over into the legal system as well. From 1930 to 1967, two-thirds of prisoners executed in southern states were African American. And many were executed for crimes that seldom resulted in death for white prisoners—rape, for example. Between 1930 and 1972, 455 people were executed for the crime of rape, and of those 455 people, 405 were African American. Based on statistics like these, it is difficult to argue that substantial racial bias against African Americans did not exist in the U.S. judicial system before the 1970s.

But people still argue about how much of that bias remains today. Laws have been passed designed to eliminate racial bias throughout the criminal justice system, including death penalty procedures. A jury, for example, is instructed that

> [I]n considering whether a sentence of death is justified, it shall not consider the race, color, religious beliefs, national origin, or sex of the defendant or of any victim and that the jury is not to recommend a sentence of death unless it has concluded that it would recommend a sentence of death for the crime in question no matter what the race, color, religious beliefs, national origin, or sex of the defendant or of any victim may be.

The intent to eliminate racial bias is there in black and white. However, according to death penalty opponents, that intent has yet to be realized.

Defendant-Victim Racial Combinations

	White Victim	Black Victim	Latino/a Victim	Asian Victim	Native American Victim
White Defendant	426 (53.12%)	12 (1.50%)	5 (.62%)	3 (.37%)	0 (0%)
Black Defendant	178 (22.19%)	81 (10.10%)	8 (1.00%)	6 (.75%)	0 (0%)
Latino/a Defendant	28 (3.49%)	2 (.25%)	19 (2.37%)	1 (.12%)	0 (0%)
Asian Defendant	1 (.12%)	0 (0%)	0 (0%)	4 (.50%)	4 (0%)
Native American	12 (1.50%)	0 (0%)	0 (0%)	0 (0%)	1 (.12%)
Total:	645 (80.42%)	95 (11.85%)	32 (3.99%)	14 (1.75%)	1 (.12%)

Source: www.DeathRowU.S.A. (Fall 2002)

Opponents and the Race Factor

In August 2001, the United Nations Committee on the Elimination of Racial Discrimination noted what it termed a "disturbing correlation" between the race of the victim and the race of the defendant in capital sentencing. The committee urged the United States to take care to ensure that "no death penalty is imposed as a result of racial bias." The committee was referring to statistics such as the following.

Blacks and whites are the victims of murder in nearly equal numbers in the United States. Yet of the more than 700 executions from 1977 to 2001, 80 percent of the cases involved a white victim. (See chart on page 97.)

A 1990 report by the General Accounting Office titled "Death Penalty Sentencing" revealed that blacks who kill whites are nineteen times as likely to be executed as whites who kill blacks.

African Americans represent 80 percent of Maryland's murder victims. Yet when Maryland prosecutors seek the death penalty, less than 10 percent of the victims in those cases are black. Also, nine of the thirteen men on Maryland's death row in 2002 were black, and all but one of their victims was white.

Blacks account for only 25 percent of Alabama's population. Yet from 1976 to 2000, 43 percent of

death row inmates and 71 percent of those actually executed were black.

Death penalty opponents insist that these and other statistics reveal that according to the U.S. criminal justice system, an African-American's life is worth considerably less than a white person's.

Supporters and the Race Factor

According to capital punishment supporters, however, the death penalty system does not discriminate against African Americans. The disparity that exists between the proportion of blacks who receive the death penalty as opposed to whites is not the result of racial bias on the part of the people involved in the death penalty system, they say. Instead, it results from the fact that African Americans commit a disproportionate number of crimes in general and of violent crimes in particular.

The chance of a white person going to prison sometime during his lifetime is 2.5 percent as opposed to 16.2 percent for an African American.

In 1996, 42 percent of death row inmates were African American, more than three times the percentage of African Americans in the U.S. population. But African Americans committed 43.2 percent of violent crimes that year, including 54.9 percent of all murders.

According to the U.S. Justice Department, whites arrested for murder are more likely to be sentenced to death than African Americans. (See chart below.)

In terms of actual executions, white death row prisoners are more likely to be executed than African-American death row prisoners. From **1977** to **1996**, **13.8** percent of whites on death row were executed as opposed to only **9.7** percent of African Americans.

People under sentence of death, by race, 1968–2000

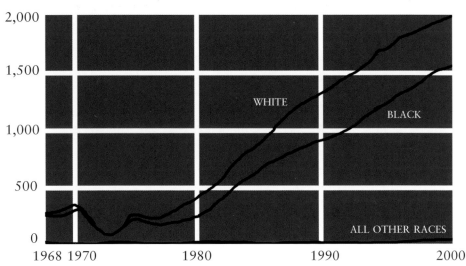

Number under sentence of death
on December 31 of each year

Source: www.DeathPenaltyU.S.A.

The crime itself is the issue in capital sentencing, not the victim's race, supporters say.

Between 92 and 97 percent of murders involve whites killing whites or blacks killing blacks. Of the small number of interracial killings, nearly all involve blacks killing whites.

Black-on-black murders are likely to involve angry confrontations between people who know each other. These kinds of murders are classified as capital crimes only rarely.

The killers involved in black-on-white murders, however, seldom know the victims. These murders are generally committed during the course of a felony, such as robbery, and often by a repeat offender. These aggravated sorts of murders are likely to be classified as capital crimes and to lead to a sentence of death.

From these and other statistics, the U.S. Department of Justice has concluded that there is "no evidence that minority defendants are subjected to bias or otherwise disfavored in decisions concerning capital punishment."

The Poverty Factor

Most of the people on any state's death row at any given time will have little money. To hire an experienced defense lawyer for a death penalty case costs a great deal—anywhere between $100 and $500 an hour and more.

Some states, such as New York and New Jersey, have made provisions for supplying, free of charge, experienced legal representation for capital defendants who cannot afford to pay a lawyer.

Other states, however, have not set aside adequate funds to cover the cost of a lawyer experienced in capital cases for defendants who can't pay. Death penalty opponents see this as a strong reason for abolishing capital punishment.

Opponents and the Poverty Factor

Opponents agree with a death row prisoner who remarked that when it comes to capital punishment, it's the people without the capital who get the punishment. Sister Helen Prejean has served as spiritual counsel to death row prisoners. In a 1995 speech in Albany, New York, she said:

> **The death penalty is a poor person's issue. Always remember that: after all the rhetoric goes on in the legislative assemblies, in the end, when the deck is cast out, it is the poor who are selected to die in this country. In the history of the death penalty it has always been that way.**

Scott Atlas, a defense attorney in death penalty cases, describes the disadvantage of lack of funds: "When people can afford quality counsel there is a lower conviction rate and a much lower rate of receiving the death penalty. If you can afford your own lawyer, your chances go up dramatically."

Most capital defendants have nowhere near the funds needed to hire an attorney experienced in death penalty cases. The Supreme Court has ruled that all capital defendants must have legal representation, and if they cannot afford to pay an attorney, then the court must appoint and pay for one. But in some states the court-appointed attorney often has little or no experience in capital trials, is paid a fraction of what lawyers experienced in capital cases normally receive, and has little or no time to prepare a client's defense.

The Massachusetts Council of Churches issued a 1997 statement that sums up the problem this way:

> **It is an historical, well-documented fact that those who suffer the death penalty are chosen not only by the nature of their crimes, but also by the color of their skin, the size of their bank accounts to purchase legal services, and the skills of their legal counsels. This discrimination against ethnic minorities and the poor is another reason for eliminating this extreme penalty.**

Supporters and the Poverty Factor

The fact that poor people receive most of the death sentences is not the fault of the death penalty system, say death penalty supporters. The poor have always filled the death rows of all nations at all times simply because the poor commit most of the violent crimes. This is a fact of life that abolishing the death penalty will not change. The Supreme Court has seen to it that all capital defendants, regardless of ability to pay, receive legal representation with access to expert witnesses and investigative services. And the Court has left it to individual state legislatures to provide this representation. The fact that some states have allocated more money to provide better representation for poor defendants than other states is a reflection of the wishes of voters in those states. It is not an indication of bias on the part of the people involved in the death penalty system, supporters say.

The Geography Factor

Each state that allows the death penalty has its own unique standards for defining what constitutes a capital crime. Each state and each county within that state also has its own unique history in regard to the death penalty. Some of these jurisdictions have a history of applying the death penalty liberally and decisively. Others are known for applying it sparingly and with great reluctance. These facts show that who gets the death penalty and who does not depends not just on what crime was committed but where it was committed. (See chart on page 105.)

Opponents and the Geography Factor

The southern states of Alabama, Arkansas, Florida, Georgia, Louisiana, Mississippi, North and South Carolina, Oklahoma, Tennessee, Texas, and Virginia contain roughly 26 percent of the nation's population. If the death penalty were fairly applied, these states would account for roughly 26 percent of the nation's executions.

Instead, between 1976 and 1995, they accounted for 79 percent of executions. Historically, southern states have elected more aggressive prosecutors and set aside more money for trying capital cases than states in other parts of the nation.

Among these southern states, Texas stands out. Between 1977 and 2001, Texas, with only 6 percent of the nation's population, executed 245 prisoners, one-third of the nation's total, more than any other state. In the first four months of 2002, Texas accounted for ten of the twenty-three executions carried out nationwide.

Within the state of Texas, one particular county stands out. Harris County, which contains Houston, leads the nation in death sentences handed out and carried out by a single jurisdiction. Between 1996 and 2001, fifty-five murderers were sent to death row in Harris County, while neighboring Dallas

Prisoners executed
by jurisdiction, 1930–December 31, 2000

Number Executed:

Jurisdiction	Since 1930	Since 1977[a]
United States, total	4,542	683
Texas	536	239
Georgia	389	23
New York	329	0
California	300	8
North Carolina	279	16
Florida	220	50
South Carolina	187	25
Ohio	173	1
Virginia	173	81
Louisiana	159	26
Alabama	158	23
Mississippi	158	4
Pennsylvania	155	3
Arkansas	141	23
Missouri	108	46
Kentucky	105	2
Illinois	102	12
Tennessee	94	1
Oklahoma	90	30
New Jersey	74	0
Maryland	71	3
Arizona	60	22
Washington	50	3
Indiana	48	7
Colorado	48	1
District of Columbia[b]	40	0
West Virginia[b]	40	0
Nevada	37	8
Federal system	33	0
Massachusetts	27	0
Delaware	23	11
Oregon	21	2
Connecticut	21	0
Utah	19	6
Iowa[b]	18	0
Kansas	15	0
Montana	8	2
Wyonming	8	1
New Mexico	8	0
Nebraska	7	3
Idaho	4	1
Vermont[b]	4	0
New Hampshire	1	0
South Dakota	1	0
Wisconsin	0	0
Rhode Island[b]	0	0
North Dakota[b]	0	0
Minnesota[b]	0	0
Michigan[b]	0	0
Maine[b]	0	0
Hawaii[b]	0	0
Alaska[b]	0	0

[a]Executions in the United Staes resumed in 1977.
[b]State did not authorize the death penalty as of December 31, 2000.

Source: U.S. Department of Justice, Bureau of Justice Statistics, *Capital Punishment* 2000, Bulletin NCJ 190598 (Washington, DC: U.S. Department of Justice, December 2001), p. 10 Table 10. Table adapted by SOURCEBOOK staff.

County, with a higher murder rate, sent only twenty-three.

Harris County is by no means the only jurisdiction with a high death penalty rate. In one county in Ohio, a murderer is seven times more likely to get the death penalty than in the state as a whole. Nationwide, fifteen counties, which together have only one-ninth of the population of death penalty states, account for nearly one-third of all executions.

If the place where a murder is committed is as important a factor in determining whether a murderer gets the death penalty as the murder itself, then capital punishment cannot be said to be fairly applied. Therefore, it should be abolished.

Supporters and the Geography Factor

The fact that the death penalty is not uniformly applied across states and counties is not the fault of the death penalty system. To insist that all the counties in all thirty-eight death penalty states apply the death penalty uniformly is to insist on the impossible. The federal government does not control how the death penalty is applied in the states. Each state and county has its own procedures. Money is more available in some jurisdictions than in others. Prosecutors are more aggressive in some jurisdictions than in others. These basic facts of life are not going to change. In a democracy where the individual states have a strong say in making and enforcing laws, they are a consequence of the system. They do not constitute reasons for abolishing the death penalty, supporters say.

10
Innocence

"Reasonable people disagree about the death penalty, but nobody can disagree that society should take extreme care to avoid executing innocent people."

These words from a June 18, 2002, *Washington Post* editorial bring up two life-and-death questions central to the death penalty debate:

Have innocent persons been executed in the past?

Have innocent persons ever been sent to death row?

The first question is all but impossible to answer conclusively. Once the prisoner is put to death, no more appeals are filed, no more witnesses are interviewed, no more investigations are conducted. In the eyes of the courts, the case is closed forever.

While it may not be possible to prove that an innocent prisoner was executed, we can examine a likely instance to discover the reasons why this might have happened in the past and might happen in the future.

The Case of Brian Baldwin

Brian Baldwin, eighteen, and Edward Horsley, seventeen, escaped from a North Carolina youth detention center in March 1977. Shortly after their escape, they hitched a ride. The driver was a sixteen-year-old girl, Naomi Rolon. Together, the three drove west to Alabama.

Exactly what happened after that will never be known with absolute certainty, but the most likely scenario is: somewhere along the road, the car stopped and Baldwin got out. Then Rolon and Horsley drove off, leaving Baldwin on his own. Sometime after that, with Baldwin miles away on his own, Horsley bludgeoned Naomi Rolon to death.

Horsley and Baldwin were later separately captured by police. At first, Horsley claimed Baldwin was Rolon's killer, but strong forensic evidence showed otherwise. The blows that ended Naomi Rolon's life were struck by a left-handed assailant, and Horsley was left-handed, while Baldwin was right-handed. And the clothing Horsley was wearing when police picked him up was blood-stained, while Baldwin's was not.

The prosecution, meanwhile, had strong evidence of its own: Baldwin's signed confession. Later, Baldwin would insist that he was innocent and that police had beaten and tortured him until he signed a statement confessing to Naomi Rolon's murder.

Brian Baldwin was black. In *Batson* v. *Kentucky*, 1986, the U.S. Supreme Court reaffirmed that intentionally excluding jurors solely on the basis of race is unconstitutional. But that decision came a decade too late for Brian Baldwin. Prosecutors were able to exclude all African Americans from the jury in Baldwin's trial—in a county where 46 percent of the residents were black.

The

SCOTTSBORO BOYS
MUST NOT DIE!

MASS SCOTTSBORO DEFENSE MEETING

At St. Mark's M. E. Church
137th Street and St. Nicholas Avenue

Friday Eve., April 14th, 8 P. M.

Protest the infamous death verdict rendered by
an all-white jury at Decatur, Alabama against
HAYWOOD PATTERSON

The Meeting will be addressed by:
Mrs. JANIE PATTERSON, mother of Haywood Patterson,
victim of the lynch verdict; SAMUEL LEIBOWITZ, chief counsel for the defense; JOSEPH BRODSKY, defense counsel;
WILLIAM PATTERSON, National Secretary of the I. L. D.;
RICHARD B. MOORE; Dr. LORENZO KING; WM. KELLEY
of the Amsterdam News; and others.

**THUNDER YOUR INDIGNATION AGAINST THE JUDICIAL MURDER
OF INNOCENT NEGRO CHILDREN !**

COME TO THE MASS PROTEST MEETING
AT ST. MARK'S M. E. CHURCH
137th Street and St. Nicholas Avenue

FRIDAY EVENING, APRIL 14th, 8 P. M.

Emergency Scottsboro Defense Committee
119 West 135th Street, New York City

Nine Innocent Men

In March 1931, nine young men were jailed in Alabama, charged with raping two young women. The defendants, who became known as the Scottsboro Boys, were innocent, but none of them had the money to hire a lawyer to fight the prosecution's case against them.

After the Supreme Court's 1963 ruling in *Gideon* v. *Wainright*, no defendant could go to trial without a lawyer. But Gideon came three decades too late for the Scottsboro Boys, and the nine young men were tried without benefit of competent counsel. The trials were tainted with racism from the start. Southern states had a notorious history of executing black men for raping white women, and the two alleged victims were white, while the nine defendants were black. All-white juries found eight of the nine guilty, and sentenced them to die in the electric chair.

The case drew publicity and protests around the world. Eventually the two "victims" admitted that the rapes had never taken place, and the Alabama courts conceded that the prisoners were in fact innocent. By this time, the eight innocent Scottsboro Boys had collectively spent eighty years in prison for crimes they did not commit, and only narrowly escaped being put to death in Alabama's electric chair.

Baldwin was found guilty and sentenced to death in a trial that took less than two days, from jury selection to sentencing. The jury never considered the strong forensic evidence in Baldwin's favor because his court-appointed lawyer never presented it. During the trial, Baldwin's lawyer presented no witnesses and no evidence on behalf of his client.

Years later, in 1985, Horsley signed a statement admitting that Baldwin "was not present at any point before or after the murder of Naomi occurred. In fact he was not even aware that she had been killed until after we were arrested and the dead body was recovered that night in Monroeville."

But appeals courts refused to permit Horsley's statement to be introduced as new evidence, and on June 18, 1999, Brian Baldwin was put to death in Alabama's electric chair.

Was Edward Horsley telling the truth? Was Brian Baldwin innocent of the murder of Naomi Rolon? The evidence points strongly in that direction. But Baldwin's innocence will never be proven in a court of law. There has never been an official, documented case of an innocent person being executed in modern times.

But the other question—Have innocent persons ever been sent to death row?—can be answered with certainty, and the answer is yes. Here is one example.

The Case of Rolando Cruz

In 1985, Rolando Cruz was found guilty of the kidnapping, rape, and murder of a ten-year-old girl, Jeanine Nicarico, in the Chicago suburb of Naperville. The evidence against Cruz consisted of statements made by Cruz himself. He told police he had "dream visions" of the crime, which partly resembled the circumstances of the crime itself. No physical evidence existed to link Cruz to the crime, only these "dream visions." Still, Cruz was found guilty and sentenced to death.

The case against Rolando Cruz began unraveling soon after he landed on death row. Brian Dugan, a convicted rapist-murderer, confessed to police that he was the real killer of Jeanine Nicarico. But police and prosecutors successfully fought to keep Dugan's confession out of court to make sure that Cruz remained on death row.

After nearly a decade of appeals, the court finally agreed to accept Dugan's confession. Also in Cruz's favor were two other new pieces of evidence. A police officer who had provided crucial evidence against Cruz in the original trial admitted that he had lied under oath, and DNA evidence from the crime scene, which could now be analyzed because of advances in forensic technology, showed that Cruz could not have been the rapist.

In 1995, after serving nearly twelve years in prison, Rolando Cruz was found innocent, exonerated, and set free. Cruz's conviction was one of more than one hundred death penalty convictions that have been reversed since the 1970s.

Four Fundamental Problems

Taken together, the Baldwin and Cruz cases illustrate four fundamental problems in the criminal justice system that can allow innocent defendants to be sent to death row:

> **incompetent counsel**
> **false confessions**
> **faulty eyewitness testimony**
> **problems with forensic evidence**

Before examining these problems, it should be noted that they are by no means confined to the death penalty system. These problems affect all levels of the criminal justice system, from the pettiest of crimes to the most serious.

Incompetent Counsel

The court must appoint an attorney for any defendant who cannot afford one. In the case of Brian Baldwin, the court-appointed attorney was not up to the difficult task of handling a capital defense.

But at least Baldwin's lawyer remained awake through his trial. Calvin J. Burdine's attorney kept falling asleep. In 1984, Burdine was convicted of murder and sentenced to death. In 2002, he won the right to a new trial because his court-appointed lawyer had slept through much of the 1984 trial and the sentencing phase that followed.

Other court-appointed lawyers have been observed sleeping through capital trials. A Houston, Texas, newspaper reporter described the behavior of one defense lawyer during a capital trial this way: "His mouth kept falling open and his head lolled back on his shoulders, and then he awakened just long enough to catch himself and sit upright. Then it happened again. And again. And again."

One study found that of the prisoners who are freed after being falsely convicted of a capital crime, 27 percent were on death row primarily because of inadequate legal help. The American Bar Association (ABA), an organization of legal professionals with some 400,000 members, has called for a moratorium on executions until reforms are made: "[G]rossly unqualified and undercompensated lawyers who have nothing like the support necessary to mount an adequate defense are often appointed to represent capital clients." The ABA called upon death-penalty states to raise their standards for court-appointed counsel in order to reduce the risk of executing innocent people.

Since the ABA's call for reform in 1997, some states have put in place standards that ensure competent legal counsel for capital prisoners. But many have not. A June 18, 2002, *Washington Post* editorial reported that "Many states provide such low-quality lawyering to the accused that egregious miscarriages of justice are inevitable."

False Confessions

If Edward Horsley's statement that Brian Baldwin was innocent was true, then Baldwin was executed because he confessed to a crime he did not commit. It is known that innocent people sometimes make false confessions that lead to convictions. Jerry Frank Townsend was one. This twenty-seven-year-old man who suffered from mental retardation admitted to six murders and a rape in 1979. He served twenty-two years in a Florida prison before new forensic evidence helped to exonerate him in 2001.

Why do people admit to crimes they did not commit? Some are physically coerced by police. This is what Brian Baldwin claimed happened to him. Others cave in under hours of continuous interrogation, too frightened or exhausted to go on resisting, sometimes agreeing to confess to a lesser crime, such as manslaughter, that will save them from execution. Some, such as Jerry Frank Townsend, give in because of a diminished mental capacity that allows police interrogators to persuade them that they may have committed the crime without knowing it.

Faulty Eyewitness Testimony

Eyewitness testimony in capital cases can amount to powerful evidence. But eyewitness testimony is often flawed.

Edward Horsley's alleged eyewitness account of the murder of Naomi Rolon was flawed for personal reasons, to shift guilt away from himself. And what about eyewitness testimony from people who were not directly involved in the crime, who have nothing to gain? Their testimony is often less than accurate as well. As one commentator wrote:

Human memory, after all, is not a video recorder, faithfully keeping an impartial record of all that its eyes see. Memory cannot be separated from human emotion—fear, rage, denial. It records, too often, what it wants to see. In rape cases, especially, eyewitness identifications are often unreliable.

The consequences of flawed eyewitness testimony can be tragic. A study of the trials of eighty-six death row inmates who were eventually exonerated found that faulty eyewitness identification played a significant part in more than half the false convictions, making it the most common factor in sending these innocent defendants to death row.

Problems with Forensic Evidence

Forensic evidence is scientific evidence presented in court to help determine guilt or innocence in criminal cases. As noted earlier, key forensic evidence that might have saved Brian Baldwin was never introduced. In many cases, though, forensic evidence does successfully help solve crimes, but not when that evidence is flawed. In May 2001, the Oklahoma State Bureau of Investigation began reviewing forensic evidence that may prove to be invalid in more than 1,000 criminal cases. The review began after defense attorneys and forensic scientists began questioning the work of Oklahoma City police chemist Joyce Gilchrist. After a preliminary study uncovered significant problems in 130 of 800 cases reviewed, Gilchrist was fired.

Gilchrist's forensic work involved both analyzing crime scene evidence and testifying to the results in court as an expert witness. Did her work result in innocent men being sent to death row? Between 1980 and 2001, twenty-three inmates were sent to Oklahoma's death row due partly to Gilchrist's forensic analysis and her testimony in court. By May 2001, eleven of those inmates already had been executed, with the remaining twelve still waiting on death row. Meanwhile, the review of Gilchrist's cases continues.

The Role of DNA

Some death row prisoners have been exonerated thanks to DNA testing. Among them was Ray Krone. His story shows why opponents see deoxyribonucleic acid (DNA) as an important new weapon in their fight against capital punishment. In 1992, Krone was found guilty of the murder of Kim Ancona, a Phoenix waitress, and sentenced to death. Krone's conviction was due largely to the inclusion of forensic analysis by an expert in bite marks, who determined that Krone's teeth matched the pattern in a wound on Ancona's arm.

At the time of Krone's trial, DNA technology was not advanced enough to produce a distinct DNA profile from the saliva the killer left on Ancona's arm. DNA, the genetic material contained in nearly all of the 100 trillion cells in a person's body, is as unique as fingerprints. No two people, with the exception of identical twins, have the same DNA profile.

By 2002, DNA technology had improved, and Krone's

attorney persuaded a judge to submit preserved saliva samples from Ancona's wound for forensic testing. This time a distinct DNA profile came back—a profile that did not match Krone's. But it did match the DNA profile of Kenneth Phillips. Authorities found the match by checking DNA profiles of other violent criminals in a federal database. Phillips, who was in prison for another crime, was charged with the murder of Kim Ancona, and Ray Krone was exonerated.

Krone was released from prison in April 2002 after serving ten years, three of them on death row. On the occasion of Krone's release, a *Washington Post* editorial stated: "Once again it becomes clear that prosecutors and juries can be absolutely sure they've got the right man—and be absolutely wrong. In the face of this knowledge, it takes a lot of arrogance to permit a penalty that cannot be undone."

Innocence Projects and DNA

In 1992, at the Benjamin N. Cardozo School of Law at Yeshiva University in New York City, the first Innocence Project was launched. More soon followed. Today there are dozens of Innocence Projects in law schools nationwide. The project rests on two assumptions: innocent people are on death row or are serving long prison sentences for violent crimes they did not commit, and some of these innocent people could be exonerated by the presentation of new evidence or by DNA testing of evidence from the crime scene. Since capital murder cases often involve sexual assault, the semen sample from the perpetrator may still be on file at a crime lab and available for testing.

The process works this way. Inmates answer a questionnaire, telling the project why they are in prison and why they believe they are innocent. Project members—law professors and their students—review the questionnaires and select those that look promising. If police are still holding DNA evidence from the crime scene, project members work on the inmate's behalf, free of charge, to have the case reopened and the DNA evidence tested.

Why wasn't the evidence tested for the original trial? DNA testing wasn't introduced into the criminal justice system until the mid- to late 1980s. For some of these inmates, their trials were over by then and they had already been sentenced. For others, the DNA evidence was too small or too damaged to be tested as evidence for the original trial, but recent technological advances make it possible to test that evidence now, as in the case of Ray Krone. For still others, the DNA evidence went untested due to incompetence on the part of the original trial lawyer.

Ray Krone was the hundredth prisoner exonerated by DNA testing. Scott Wallace, director of defender services at National Legal Aid and Defender Association in Washington, D.C., said, "It all comes back to three little letters: D-N-A. Science has convinced the public and prosecutors that the criminal justice system is far more fallible than they had ever expected."

Lawmakers Respond

Lawmakers have responded to the DNA-based exonerations by changing laws. Seventeen states have passed legislation designed to give inmates easier access to post-conviction DNA testing. Two death penalty states, New York and Illinois, changed laws in order to allow any inmate with a legitimate claim to innocence to demand DNA evidence testing.

In the year 2000, two lawmakers in particular responded with deep concern. Governors George Ryan of Illinois and Parris Glendening of Maryland ordered a moratorium, a temporary halt, on executions in their states.

Governor Ryan acted in January 2000 after the *Chicago*

Tribune reported that since 1977, one-half of all capital convictions in Illinois had been reversed because of fundamental errors, including incompetent defense counsel, flawed forensic evidence, and all-white juries. Most of these reversals resulted in the inmate's sentence being commuted to life in prison, while thirteen of these Illinois death row inmates were found to have been falsely convicted. They were exonerated and released from prison.

Governor Ryan had once been an outspoken death penalty supporter. "I believed some crimes were so heinous that the only proper way of protecting society was execution," he said. "I saw a nation in the grip of increasing crime rates; and tough sentences, more jails, the death penalty—that was good government."

But then came the *Tribune* report. "Thirteen times innocent men were exonerated after rotting on Death Row for years," Governor Ryan said. "For that to happen even once is unjust and for that to happen 13 times is shameful and beyond comprehension." In declaring the moratorium on January 31, 2000, he said, "I cannot support a system which, in its administration, has proved so fraught with error, and has come so close to the ultimate nightmare, the state's taking of innocent life."

Governor Ryan ordered a commission of criminal justice experts to study the system and recommend action. The commission's completed study listed eighty-five recommended reforms, including a drastic reduction in the kinds and number of aggravating factors that can classify a crime as capital and result in capital punishment.

When the Illinois state legislature failed to institute any of the recommended reforms, Governor Ryan took action. On January 14, 2003, two days before his term as governor was to end, he used powers granted to the governor by the Illinois constitution to empty Illinois' death row. Governor Ryan pardoned four death row inmates who claimed that they had been tortured into false murder confessions. The other 156 death row inmates and 11 more who had been sentenced to death but were awaiting hearings had their sentences commuted to life in prison without possibility of parole. In a speech at Northwestern University Law School in Chicago announcing his decision, Ryan said, "Our capital system is haunted by the demon of error, error in determining guilt, error in determining who among the guilty deserves to die. Because of all of these reasons, I'm commuting the sentence of all death row inmates."

Governor Glendening declared the Maryland moratorium in May 2002, citing as his primary reason possible racial bias in sentencing. He ordered the moratorium to remain in effect until a special study could be completed on whether African-American and Hispanic prisoners were being unjustly singled out for capital punishment. "It is imperative that I, as well as our citizens, have complete confidence that the legal process involved in capital cases is fair and impartial," he said.

The U.S. Congress itself responded to concerns about the death penalty. One response was a congressional bill known as the Innocence Protection Act, introduced by Senator Patrick Leahy of Vermont. Leahy's bill proposes to do the following:

(1) Ensure that convicted offenders are afforded an opportunity to prove their innocence through DNA testing; (2) help states to provide competent legal services at every stage of a death penalty prosecution; (3) enable those who can prove their innocence to recover some measure of compensation for their unjust

incarceration; and (4) provide the public with more re-
liable and detailed information regarding the administration of the nation's capital punishment laws.

One section of the bill requires states to make DNA
testing available to inmates who demand it or else lose federal money for DNA-related programs. Leahy's bill is one
example of congressional response to growing concern
over problems with the death penalty.

Meanwhile, the debate between death penalty opponents and supporters over the likelihood of innocent prisoners being executed continues.

Opponents and the Innocence Issue

There can be no guarantee that innocent prisoners have
not been executed in the past and will not be executed in
the future, opponents say. Therefore, the death penalty
must be abolished. It is the responsibility of the criminal
justice system to protect innocent citizens, not kill them.
The execution of even one innocent person ought to be un-
acceptable. The numerous DNA-based exonerations make
it clear that while some innocent inmates have been saved
from death, more—perhaps a great many more—remain
on death row awaiting execution. Here is how two U.S.
Supreme Court justices feel about the possibility of the innocent being executed:

**Justice Sandra Day O'Connor, in a speech to the
American Bar Association in July, 2001: "If statistics are any indication, the system may well be allowing some innocent defendants to be executed."**

Former Justice Thurgood Marshall: "No matter how careful courts are, the possibility of perjured testimony, mistaken honest testimony, and human error remain all too real. We have no way of judging how many innocent persons have been executed, but we can be certain that there were some."

Mistakes that send innocent men to prison for life can be corrected, say opponents, but not mistakes that send innocent men to the execution chamber. As one former judge said, "If you find out that you've executed an innocent person, you don't go to the same cemetery, dig up the coffin, open up and say, 'Sorry, we've made a mistake.'"

Supporters and the Innocence Issue

Death penalty supporters see DNA-based exonerations a different way. In their eyes, exonerations show that the death penalty system, while imperfect, does everything humanly possible to eliminate chances of fatal mistakes. Advances in DNA testing technologies since the 1980s have strengthened the capital punishment system, not weakened it, supporters say. An April 18, 2002, *Wall State Journal* editorial stated: "The use of DNA evidence was supposed to make death-penalty convictions seem illegitimate, and it has done a service by exposing some earlier injustice. But the accuracy of DNA testing means we can now be more confident than ever that only the guilty will be executed." South Carolina district attorney John Justice added that "the reversals prove that the system works."

These DNA-based exonerations came through the appeals system, which allows capital prisoners an average of ten years to correct any mistakes with their verdict or sentencing, supporters point out. Law professor Paul Cassell of the University of Utah calls the reversals resulting from the lengthy capital appeals system "a consequence of having a system that's very careful," not evidence that the system is error-prone. Cassell cites the results of an extensive study on the death penalty system released in 2000. "After reviewing twenty-three years of capital cases, the study's authors (like other researchers) were unable to find a single case in which an innocent person was executed. Thus, the most important error rate—the rate of mistaken executions—is zero."

No one wants to see an innocent person executed, say supporters. But, as former prosecutor William Kunkle says, "It is not humanly possible to design a system that is perfect. And if people are not prepared for the eventuality that human institutions are going to make mistakes, then they shouldn't support the death penalty, and they shouldn't elect legislators who support it."

Polls show that while Americans accept the fact that innocent people are sometimes found guilty of murder, a majority still support the death penalty.

Conclusion

As mentioned earlier, the United States is the only Western nation that still practices capital punishment. In terms of human rights, this puts America in questionable company. Countries the United States often criticizes for human rights violations, such as Iran, Iraq, and China, still have the death penalty. Meanwhile, countries with admirable human rights records, such as Canada, Sweden, and France, have all abolished it.

In 2000, the fourteen countries in the European Union (EU) voted to refuse to extradite accused murderers to any death penalty nation, including, of course, the United States. Some EU leaders who see capital punishment as inhumane wonder why the United States refuses to give it up. Henry LeClerc, president of the Human Rights League in Paris, says: "For us, what the Americans are doing is completely incomprehensible, that such an advanced country can be involved in such an act of barbarism."

Why does the United States still practice capital punishment?

Part of the answer lies in national crime rates, which typically run from four to ten times higher in the United States than in the EU nations. When the United States did stop executions, from 1966 to 1977, crime rates soared. When executions began again, crime rates dropped. The American public, confronted with high rates of violent crime relative to other Western nations, understandably responds with calls for stricter crime controls, including capital punishment. Though the percentage varies from poll to poll, the majority of the American public continues to support capital punishment.

But to label the United States "barbaric" for supporting and practicing capital punishment, as Henry LeClerc does, is an unfairly harsh judgment. As we have seen, U.S. courts sentence only a tiny percentage of violent criminals to death, and execute only a few of those, and only after an appeals process that averages ten years. And then executions are greeted with protests, even when the prisoner being executed is mass murderer Timothy McVeigh. While capital punishment is still practiced in America, it is practiced with considerable restraint and reluctance.

Notes

Foreword

p. 8, par. 1, "Defiant McVeigh Dies in Silence." BBC News. June 11, 2001. news.bbc.co.uk/hi/english/world/americas/newsid_ 1382000/138260.stm. (Accessed April 29, 2003.)

p. 8, par. 1,"Protester Turnout Low for McVeigh Execution." CNN.com. June 12, 2001. www.cnn.com/2001/LAW/06/11/ mcveigh.protests. (Accessed April 29, 2003.)

p. 8, par. 2,"Defiant McVeigh Dies in Silence."

p. 8, par. 2, "Protester Turnout Low for McVeigh Execution."

p. 8, par. 3,"Defiant McVeigh Dies in Silence."

p. 8, par. 3, "Death Sentence 2002." deathsentence2002.home.att.net/ quotes.html. (Accessed July 11, 2002.)

Chapter 1

p. 11, par. 1, Scalia, Antonin. "God's Justice and Ours." *First Things*. May 2002. www.firstthings.com/ftissues/ft0205/articles/scalia.html. (Accessed April 29, 2003.)

p. 12, par. 3, Scott-Kilvert, I. *The Rise and Fall of Athens. Nine Greek Lives by Plutarch*. New York: Penguin Books, 1960. http://mkatz.web. wesleyan.edu/Images2/cciv243.Solon.html. (Accessed April 29, 2003.)

p. 16, par. 1, Nolan, John. "Serial Killer Set to Die in Ohio." Softcon Internet Communications, April 25, 2002. www.softcom.net/ webnews/wed/do/Acoleman-crime-spree.RMD3_CAP.html. (Accessed April 29, 2003.)

p. 17, "U.S. Code Collection." Legal Information Institute. www4.law. cornell.edu/uscode/18/17.html. (Accessed April 29, 2003.)

p. 18, par. 3, McGunagle, Fred. "Mark David Chapman: The Man Who Killed John Lennon." *The Crime Library*. www.crimelibrary.com/ classics4/chapman. (Accessed June 2, 2002.)

p. 19, par. 3, U.S. Supreme Court. *Daryl Renard Atkins, Petitioner v. Virginia*. June 20, 2002. www.caselaw.lp.findlaw.com/cgibin/getcase. pl?court=US&navby=case&vol=000&invol=00-8452. (Accessed April 29, 2003.)

p. 21, par. 3, Phillips, Robert Anthony. "No Gender Equality on Death Row." APBnews.com. February 26, 2002. www.apbnews.com/cjsystem/ findingjustice/2000/02/26/women0226_02.html. (Accessed April 11, 2002.)

p. 21, par. 4, Ibid.

p. 21, par. 5, Associated Press. "Yates' Attorneys Focus on Sentencing." *The New York Times*. March 13, 2002. www.nytimes.com/aponline/ national/AP-Children-Slain.html. (Accessed April 29, 2003.)

p. 22, par. 4, U.S. Supreme Court. *Stanford v. Kentucky*. June 26, 1989. caselaw.lp.findlaw.com/scripts/getcase.pl?court=US&vol= 492&invol=361. (Accessed April 29, 2003.)

p. 22, par. 6, Rimer, Sara, and Raymond Bonner. "Young and Condemned/ A Special Report." *The New York Times*. August 22, 2000. www.deathpenaltyinfo.org/NYT-Juv.html. (Accessed April 29, 2003.)

p. 23, par. 2, U.S. Supreme Court. *In Re Kevin Nigel Stanford*. October 21, 2002. www.medill.northwestern.edu/docket/stanford. html. (Accessed April 29, 2003.)

Chapter 2

p. 28, par. 1, Tolson, Mike. "A Deadly Distinction." *Houston Chronicle*. February 5, 2001. www.chron.com/cs/CDA/printstory.hts/special/ penalty/816416. (Accessed April 29, 2003.)

p. 28, par. 2, U.S. Supreme Court. *Gideon v. Wainwright*. March 18, 1963. www2.law.cornell.edu/cgi-bin/foliocgi.exe/historic/query=[group+ 372+u!2Es!2E+335!3A]^[group+citemenu!3A]^[level+case+citation! 3A]^[group+notes!3A]/doc/{@21}/hit_headings/words=4/hits_only? (Accessed April 29, 2003.)

p. 28, par. 4, Berlow, Alan. "The Wrong Man," *Atlantic Monthly*, November 1999, www.theatlantic.com/issues/99nov/99/ wrongman.htm. (Accessed May 3, 2003.)

p. 31, par. 3, Lifton, Robert Jay, and Greg Mitchell. *Who Owns Death?* New York: William Morrow, 2000, p. 161.

p. 31, par. 4, Berlow.

p. 33, par. 3, "Capital Punishment in Tennessee: A Brief Timeline History & Overview of the Legal Process." tscaoc.tsc.state.tn.us/geninfo/ Publications/dpbrochure.pdf. (Accessed August 7, 2002.)

Chapter 3

p. 34, par. 1, Lifton, Robert Jay, and Greg Mitchell. *Who Owns Death?* New York: William Morrow, 2000, p. 252.

p. 37, par. 2, Leuchter, Fred A. "Execution by Hanging Operation and Instruction Manual." Department of Correction, State of Delaware. May 1, 1990. www.angelfire.com/f13/starke/hanging.html. (Accessed May 17, 2002.)

p. 37, par. 3, Ibid.

p. 41, par. 1, The Supreme Court of Georgia. S01A1041. *Dawson v. The State* / S01A12010. Moore v. The State." October 5, 2001. http://216.239.51.100/search?q=cache:UZE4kzjDNNIC:www.sound portraits.org/data/on-air/ga_decision.pdf+georgia+supreme+court+ excruciating&hl=en&ie=UTF-8. (Accessed April 29, 2003.)

p. 41, par. 2, "Georgia Bans Electric Chair." BBC News. October 5, 2001. news.bbc.co.uk/hi/english/world/americas/newsid_1581000/ 1581751.stm. (Accessed April 29, 2003.)

p. 43, par. 2, Kunkle, William. Interview with the author, Chicago, Illinois. July 10, 2002.

p. 43, par. 3, Lifton, p. 62.

p. 43, par. 4, Lifton, p. 96.

p. 47, par. 2, Associated Press. "Ark. Killer's Last Words: I Love You, My Babies." Court TV Online. May 3, 2000. www.courttv.com/national/ 2000/0503/arkansas_ap.html. (Accessed April 29, 2003.)

p. 47, Lowenstein, Tom. "The Burden of Execution." *The American Prospect*. December 3, 2001. www.prospect.org/print/V12/21/ lowenstein-t.html. (Accessed April 29, 2003.)

p. 47, Lifton, p. 187.

p. 47, "Dying Words of Famous People." Corsinet.com. www.corsinet.com/ braincandy/dying2.html. (Accessed April 29, 2003.)

p. 47, Banner, Stuart. *The Death Penalty: An American History*. Cambridge, MA: Harvard University Press, 2002, p. 309.

p. 47, "Dying Words of Famous People."

p. 47, "Au Revoir Les Inmates." w3.one.net/~tdaniels/cooking.html. (Accessed May 23, 2002.)

p. 47, "Au Revoir Les Inmates."

p. 47, "Reflections on a Quarter-Century of Constitutional Regulation of Capital Punishment." *The John Marshall Law Review*. vol. 30, winter 1997, p. 428.

p. 48, par. 2, Glaberson, William. "Inside a Modern Death Row, the Prisoners Can Only Wait." *The New York Times*. April 26, 2002. www.santegidio.org/pdm/news2002/12_06_02_b.htm. (Accessed April 29, 2003.)

p. 49, par. 4, Banner, p. 31.

p. 50, par. 3, Lifton, p. 172.

p. 52, par. 2, Lifton, p. 191.

p. 52, par. 3, Lifton, p. 194.

Chapter 4

p. 55, par. 1, U.S. Supreme Court. *Weems* v. *U.S.* May 2, 1910. http://caselaw.lp.findlaw.com/scripts/getcase.pl?court=us&vol=217&invol=349. (Accessed April 29. 2003.)

p. 55, par. 3, Kaminer, Wendy. *It's All the Rage: Crime and Culture*. Reading, MA: Addison-Wesley, 1995, p. 128.

p. 55, par. 3, Banner, Stuart. *The Death Penalty: An American History*. Cambridge, MA: Harvard University Press, 2002, p. 263.

p. 55, par. 3, Banner, p. 263.

p. 55, par. 4, "Reflections on a Quarter-Century of Constitutional Regulation of Capital Punishment," *The John Marshall Law Review*. vol. 30, winter 1997, p. 407.

p. 55, par. 5, Kaminer, p. 128.

p. 56, Banner, par. 3, p. 263.

Chapter 5

p. 61, par. 3, Kaminer, Wendy. *It's All the Rage: Crime and Culture*. Reading, MA: Addison-Wesley, 1995, p. 138.

p. 61, par. 3, Lowenstein, Tom. "The Burden of Execution." *The American Project*. December 3, 2001. www.prospect.org/print/u12/21/lowenstein-t.html. (Accessed April 29, 2003.)

p. 62, par. 1, Hook, Donald H., and Lothar Kahn. *Death in the Balance*. Lexington, MA: Lexington Books, 1989, back cover.

p. 62, par. 4, Lifton, Robert Jay, and Greg Mitchell. *Who Owns Death?* New York: William Morrow, 2000, p. 113.

p. 63, par. 1, Jackson, Jesse L. Sr., Jesse L. Jackson Jr., and Bruce Shapiro.

Legal Lynching: The Death Penalty and America's Future. New York: New Press, 2001, pp. 26–27.

p. 63, par. 2, Solotaroff, Ivan. *The Last Face You'll Ever See: The Private Life of the American Death Penalty.* New York: HarperCollins Publishers, 2001, p. 34.

p. 64, par. 2, "Reflections on a Quarter-Century of Constitutional Regulation of Capital Punishment," *The John Marshall Law Review.* vol. 30, winter 1997, p. 434.

p. 65, par. 1, Tolson, Mike. "Death Penalty Reforms Sought." *Houston Chronicle.* February 7, 2001. www.chron.com/cs/CDA/printstory.hts/special/penalty/816416. (Accessed April 29, 2003.)

p. 67, par. 3, U.S. Supreme Court. *Furman* v. *Georgia.* June 29, 1972. caselaw.lp.findlaw.com/scripts/getcase.pl?court=US&vol=408&invol=238. (Accessed April 29, 2003.)

p. 67, par. 4, Tolson, Mike. "A Deadly Distinction."

p. 68, par. 1, "Death Sentence 2002." deathsentence2002.home.att.net/quotes.html. (Accessed July 11, 2002.)

p. 68, par. 6, Dezhbakhsh, Hashem, Paul H. Rubin, and Joanna M. Shepherd. "Does Capital Punishment Have a Deterrent Effect? New Evidence from Post-moratorium Panel Data." February 2001, pp. 26–27. userwww.service.emory.edu/~cozden/Dezhbakhsh_01_01_paper.pdf. (Accessed April 29, 2003.)

p. 69, par. 2, "Purposes of the Death Penalty." *Focus on Law Studies,* Vol. XII, Number 2, Spring, 1997. www.abanet.org/publiced/focus/spr97pur.html. (Accessed April 29, 2003.)

Chapter 6

p. 70, par. 1, Camus, Albert. "Reflections on the Guillotine," *Resistance, Rebellion, and Death.* New York: Vintage Books, 1974, pp. 190–191.

p. 72, par. 4, Glaberson, William. "From Death Row, an Inmate Battles to Control His Case." *The New York Times.* June 24, 2002. www.humanrightsmonitor.org/article221.html. (Accessed April 29, 2003.)

p. 73, par. 1, Coen, Jeff, and Art Barnum. "Lemak Gets Life Term for Killing Her 3 Kids." *Chicago Tribune.* April 9, 2002. fact.on.ca./news/news0204/ct020409.htm. (Accessed April 29, 2003.)

p. 74, par. 1, Jackson, Jesse L. Sr., Jesse L. Jackson Jr., and Bruce Shapiro. *Legal Lynching: The Death Penalty and America's Future.* New York: New Press, 2001, pp. 31–32.

p. 74, par. 3, "News Archives—January 2000." Death Penalty Institute of Oklahoma. www.dpio.org/archives/News/News_2000_01.html. (Accessed April 29, 2003.)

p. 74, par. 4, U.S. Supreme Court. *Furman* v. *Georgia*, caselaw.p.find law.com/scripts/getcase.pl?court=US&vol=408&invol=238. (Accessed April 29, 2003.)

Chapter 7

p. 77, par. 6, "Capital Punishment." The Internet Encyclopedia of Philosophy. www.utm.edu/research/iep/c/capitalp.htm. (Accessed May 23, 2002.)

p. 78, par. 1, Van den Haag, Ernest, and John Phillips Conrad. *The Death Penalty: A Debate*. New York: Plenum Press, 1983, p. 23.

p. 78, par. 4, Lifton, Robert Jay, and Greg Mitchell. *Who Owns Death?* New York: William Morrow, 2000, p. 162.

p. 78, par. 5, Hook, Donald H., and Lothar Kahn. *Death in the Balance*. Lexington, MA: Lexington Books, 1989, p. 52.

p. 79, par. 6, "Death Sentence 2002." deathsentence2002.home. att.net/quotes.html. (Accessed July 11, 2002.)

p. 79, par. 2, "A Good Friday Appeal to End the Death Penalty." Administrative Board of the United States Conference of Catholic Bishops. April 2, 1999. www.usccb.org/sdwp/national/criminal/appeal.htm. (Accessed April 29, 2003.)

p. 79, par. 4, Jackson, Jesse L. Sr., Jesse L. Jackson Jr., and Bruce Shapiro. *Legal Lynching: The Death Penalty and America's Future*. New York: New Press, 2001, p. 88.

p. 79, par. 5, quoted in Fuller, Edmund, ed. *Thesaurus of Quotations*. New York: Crown Publishers, 1941. Quote #2832.

p. 80, par. 1, U.S. Supreme Court. *Furman* v. *Georgia*, caselaw.p.find law.com/scripts/getcase.pl?court=US&vol=408&invol=238. (Accessed April 29, 2003.)

p. 80, par. 4, U.S. Supreme Court. *Furman* v. *Georgia*, caselaw.p.find law.com/scripts/getcase.pl?court=US&vol=408&invol=238. (Accessed April 29, 2003.)

p. 82, par. 2, Lifton, ibid, p. 114.

p. 83, par. 1, Goodhart, A. L. *English Law and the Moral Law*. London: Stevens & Sons, 1953, pp. 92–93.

p. 83, par. 5, "Appeals." www.prodeathpenalty.com/Appeals.htm. (Accessed June 12, 2002.)

p. 83, par. 6, Solotaroff, Ivan. *The Last Face You'll Ever See: The Private Life of the American Death Penalty and America's Future*. New York: New Press, 2001, p. 49.

p. 84, par. 1, Berns, Walter. *For Capital Punishment: Crime and the Morality of the Death Penalty*. Lanham, MD: University Press of

America, Inc., 1991, p. 162.

p. 84, par. 2, Kunkle, personal interview.

p. 84, par. 3, Lifton, Robert Jay, and Greg Mitchell. *Who Owns Death?* New York: William Morrow, 2000, p. 252.

p. 85, par. 1, Lifton, p. 203.

p. 85, par. 2, Mills, Steve. "'84 Killer on Eve of Conviction." *Chicago Tribune*, April 25, 2002. www.chicagotribune.com/news/local/ showcase/chi-0204250300apr25.story?coll=chi%2Dnews%2Dhed. (Accessed May 12, 2002.)

p. 85, par. 2, Nolan, John. "Serial Killer Set to Die in Ohio." Softcom Internet Commnications. April 25, 2002. www.softcom.net/ webnews/wed/do/Acoleman-crime-spreeRMD3_CAP.html. (Accessed April 29, 2003.)

p. 85, par. 3, Solotaroff, p. 75.

p. 86, par. 1, Jackson, p. 80.

p. 86, par. 1, Lifton, p. 205.

p. 86, par. 2, Lifton, p. 202.

p. 86, par. 3, Lifton, p. 210.

Chapter 8

p. 88, par. 4, Rush, Benjamin. "An Enquiry into the Influence of Physical Causes upon the Moral Faculty," *Two Essays on the Mind*. New York: Brunner/Mazel, 1972, p. 36.

p. 89, par. 4, Dickens, Charles. *American Notes and Pictures from Italy*. New York: Oxford University Press, 1966, p. 100.

p. 89, par. 5, Banner, *The Death Penalty: An American History*. Cambridge, MA: Harvard University Press, 2002.

p. 91, par. 3, Chessman, Caryl. *Cell 2455 Death Row*. New York: Putnam's Sons, 1961, p. 359.

p. 92, par. 1, Bisbort, Alan. "The Curious Case of Caryl Chessman." Gadflyonline. July 9, 2001. www.gadflyonline.com/10/29/01/ ftr-caryl-chessman.html. (Accessed May 12, 2002.)

p. 93, par. 2, Wills, Garry. Review of *A Time to Die* by Tom Wicker, in *New York Review of Books*, April 3, 1975, p. 3.

Chapter 9

p. 96, par. 5, U.S. Department of Justice. "The Federal Death Penalty System: Supplementary Data, Analysis and Revised Protocols for Capital Case Review." June 6, 2001. www.usdoj.gov/dag/pubdoc/ deathpenaltystudy.htm. (Accessed April 11, 2003.)

p. 98, par. 1, "Racist Application of the Death Penalty." Worldwide

Appeals. December 2001. www.web.amnesty.org/web/wwa.nsf/
41c3ff3c0a005c9380256771004eca4c/5a19406e73ef038380256
b0c9005f06c4!OpenDocument. (Accessed April 11, 2002.)
p. 101, par. 5, U.S. Department of Justice.
p. 102, par. 4, "Religious Positions." Death Sentence 2002.
deathsentence2002.home.att.net/religious.html. (Accessed May 24, 2002.)
p. 102, par. 5, Tolson, Mike. "Between Life and Death." *Houston
Chronicle.* February 5, 2001. www.chron.com/cs/CDA/
printstory.hts/special/penalty/814496. (Accessed April 29, 2003.)
p. 103, par. 3, "In Opposition to Capital Punishment: A Statement of
the Board of Directors of the Massachusetts Council of Churches."
October 23, 1997. www.masscouncilofchurches.org/policies.htm.
(Accessed April 29, 2003.)

Chapter 10
p. 107, par. 1, "Checks on the Death Penalty." *The Washington Post.*
June 18, 2002, p. A18.
p. 110, par. 2, Vanderhoof, David. "Introduction to Criminal Justice
Exam." June 18, 1999. www.uncp.edu/home/vanderhoof/Intro-
CJ-Exam-S99.html. (Accessed April 29, 2003.)
p. 112, par. 4, Jackson, Jesse L. Sr., Jesse L. Jackson Jr., and Bruce
Shapiro. *Legal Lynching: The Death Penalty and America's Future.*
New York: New Press, 2001, p. 36.
p. 112, par. 5, "American Bar Association Calls for Moratorium on
Capital Punishment." Court TV Online. February 3, 1997.
www.courttv.com/legaldocs/rights/abacap.html.
(Accessed April 29, 2003.)
p. 113, par. 2, "Checks on the Death Penalty."
p, 114, par. 2, Tucker, Cynthia. "Promote Use of DNA Tests for All
Suspects." *Atlanta Journal-Constitution.* February 10, 2002.
www.accessatlanta.com/ajc/opinion/tucker/2002/021002.html.
(Accessed April 29, 2003.)
p. 116, par. 2, "100 Death Penalty Errors." *The Washington Post.*
April 15, 2002, p. A20.
p. 117, par. 3, Willing, Richard. "Exonerated Prisoners Are Rarely Paid
for Lost Time." *USA Today.* June 18, 2002, p. 1A.
p. 118, par. 2, Jackson, p. 115.
p. 118, par. 3, Mills, Steve, and Maurice Possley. "'We're talking about
life and death . . . not about losing an election.'" *Chicago Tribune.*
April 16, 2002. www.chicagotribune.com/news/local/showcase/
chi-0204160281 apr16story?coll=chi-news-hed.

chi-0204160281 apr16story?coll=chi-news-hed.
(Accessed April 29, 2003.)

p. 118, par. 3, "Press Release Announcing the Moratorium." Inside Out
Documentaries. January 31, 2000. www.insideout.org/documentaries/
dna/thelawryan.asp. (Accessed April 29, 2003.)

p. 119, par. 1, "The Death Penalty: 'Arbitrary and Capricious.'" Text of
speech by Governor George Ryan. *Salon.com.* January 14, 2003.
www.salon.com/news/feature/2003/01/14/ryan.html.
(Accessed April 12, 2003.)

p. 119, par. 2, "Governor Glendening Issues a Stay in the Case of Wesley
Eugene Baker." State of Maryland Governor's Press Office. May 9, 2002.
www.humanrightsmonitor.org/article221.html.
(Accessed April 29, 2003.)

p. 119, par. 3, Leahy, Patrick. "The Innocence Protection Act."
leahy.senate.gov/issues/ipa. (Accessed July 18, 2002.)

p. 120, par. 5, "The Death Penalty in 2001: Year End Report." Death
Penalty Information Center. December 2001. www.deathpenalty
info.org/whatsnew.html. (Accessed April 29, 2003.)

p. 121, par. 1, Jackson, p. 64.

p. 121, par. 2, "Support for the Death Penalty Drops." ABCNews.com.
January 5, 2002. abcnews.go.com/sections/wnt/WorldNews
Tonight/wnt010502_deathpenaltypoll_feature.html.
(Accessed April 29, 2003.)

p. 121, par. 3, "Mend It, Don't End It." *The Wall Street Journal.*
April 18, 2002, p. A12.

p. 121, par. 3, Berlow, Alan. "The Wrong Man," *Atlantic Monthly,*
November 1997, www.theatlantic.com/issues/99nov/9911
wrongman.htm. (Accessed April 29, 2003.)

p. 122, par. 1, "Execution by the Numbers." ABCNews.com.
June 12, 2000. abcnews.go.com/sections/us/DailyNews/deathpenalty
study000612.html. (Accessed April 29, 2003.)

p. 122, par. 1, Cassell, Paul G. "We're Not Executing the Innocent."
The Wall Street Journal. June 16, 2000. www.prodeathpenalty.com/
Liebman/Cassell_Innocents.htm. (Accessed April 29, 2003.)

p. 122, par. 2, Berlow.

Conclusion

p. 124, Lifton, Robert Jay, and Greg Mitchell. *Who Owns Death?*
New York: William Morrow, 2000, p. 237.

Further Information

Further Reading

Bedau, Hugo Adam. *Death Is Different: Studies in the Morality, Law and Politics of Capital Punishment.* Boston: Northeastern University Press, 1987.

Fridell, Ron. *DNA Fingerprinting: The Ultimate Identity.* New York: Franklin Watts, 2001.

Loney, Randolph. *A Dream of a Tattered Man: Stories from Georgia's Death Row.* Grand Rapids, MI: William B. Erdmans, 2001.

Prejean, Helen. *Dead Man Walking: An Eyewitness Account of the Death Penalty in the United States.* New York: Random House, 1993.

Williams, Mary. *Capital Punishment.* San Diego: Greenhaven Press, 2000.

Web Sites

The following Web sites are especially good locations for picking up information on capital punishment.

Death Penalty Information Center
www.deathpenaltyinfo.org

This multi-award-winning site includes an Internet-based "Educational Curriculum on the Death Penalty." It includes lists of Web sites for teachers and students and information on a "Teen Summit on Capital Punishment."

Pro-death penalty.com
www.prodeathpenalty.com

Most death penalty Web sites are designed and maintained by opponents. This site is an exception. Among its collections of articles and interviews, most in support of the death penalty, are essays by college and high school students, and a guide to researching material for argumentative essays on the death penalty.

Death Penalty News & Updates
web.cis.smu.edu/~deathpen

A collection of the latest news and statistics on capital punishment in the United States.

Capital Punishment: Primary Legal Materials
www.ll.georgetown.edu/lr/rs/capital.html

This site, maintained by the Georgetown University Law Library, gives access to historic legal documents relating to the death penalty.

The Moratorium Campaign
www.moratorium2000.org

This is the home site of a worldwide petition drive to abolish the death penalty in all nations. It emphasizes how people can become personally involved in abolishing capital punishment.

The History of Capital Punishment
www.helsinki.fi/~tuschano/cp

This Web site from Finland is a collection of historical documents about capital punishment from the United States and other nations.

Bibliography

Banner, Stuart. *The Death Penalty: An American History.* Cambridge, MA: Harvard University Press, 2002.

Berns, Walter. *For Capital Punishment: Crime and the Morality of the Death Penalty.* Lanham, MD: University Press of America, Inc.

Camus, Albert. *Resistance, Rebellion, and Death.* New York: Vintage Books, 1974.

Dickens, Charles. *American Notes and Pictures from Italy.* New York: Oxford University Press, 1966.

Chessman, Caryl. *Cell 2455 Death Row.* New York: Putnam's Sons, 1961.

Goodhart, A. L. *English Law and the Moral Law.* London: Stevens & Sons, 1953.

Hook, Donald H., and Lothar Kahn. *Death in the Balance*. Lexington, MA: Lexington Books, 1989.

Jackson, Jesse L. Sr., Jesse L. Jackson Jr., and Bruce Shapiro. *Legal Lynching: The Death Penalty and America's Future*. New York: New Press, 2001.

Kaminer, Wendy. *It's All the Rage: Crime and Culture*. Reading, MA: Addison-Wesley, 1995.

Lifton, Robert Jay, and Greg Mitchell. *Who Owns Death?* New York: William Morrow, 2000.

Loney, Randolph. *A Dream of a Tattered Man: Stories from Georgia's Death Row*. Grand Rapids, MI: William B. Erdmans, 2001.

Solotaroff, Ivan. *The Last Face You'll Ever See: The Private Life of the American Death Penalty*. New York: HarperCollins Publishers, 2001.

Van den Haag, Ernest and John Phillips Conrad. *The Death Penalty: A Debate*. New York: Plenum Press, 1983.

Index

Page numbers in **boldface** are illustrations, tables, and charts.

Abbott, Jack Henry, 92
actus reus, 27
African Americans
  bias against, 94–101, **97**, **100**
  executions of, **66**
  as jurors, 30
  See also Baldwin, Brian;
    Scottsboro boys
aggravating factors, 14, **27**, 32, 56
aggression, 19-20
alcohol, 71
Amnesty International, **94**
ancients, 11–12, 77–78
appeals, 10–11, 32–33, 73, 121–122
Atkins v. *Virginia*, 19
Australia, 10

Babylonians, 77
Baldwin, Brian, 108, 110, 114

Batson v. *Kentucky*, 108
Beazley, Napoleon, 23
Beccaria, Cesare, 88
Beets, Betty Lou, 21
bias. *See* executions; sentencing
Bible, 78, 79
Brennan, William J., 61
Bush, George W., 67–68

Camus, Albert, 70
Canada, 10
capital crimes (defined), 11–14,
  26–28
Catholic Church, 79
Chapman, Mark David, 18
Chessman, Caryl, 91–92
clemency, 33, 118–119
Coleman, Alton, 16, 85
confessions, 108, 113

counties, 104, 106
crime rate, 53–54, 56, 68–69, 74–75, 124
crime scene, 114–115
cruel and unusual punishment, 41, 54–57, 80
Cruz, Rolando, 110–111

Dahmer, Jeffrey, 17, 71
Darrow, Clarence, 79
Dead Man Walking, 52, 136
death row
  cost of, 65
  crowding in, 59, **58**, **59**
  inmate perceptions of, 46–48, **47**, 91
death sentences. *See* sentencing
defense attorneys (role of), 28–29, 112–113
defenses
  genetics, 19–20
  insanity, 16–17
  mental retardation, 19
deterrence
  opposition views, 70–75, **74**
  support views, 62–69
Dickens, Charles, 89
DNA, 115–117, 120, 121
Draconian Code, 11–12
drugs, 71

Edison, Thomas, 39
Eighth Amendment. *See* cruel and unusual punishment
electric chair, 38–41, **51**
Emory University, 68–69
European countries, 10, 12, 75, 123–124
evidence
  DNA, 115–117, 119–120, 121
  eyewitness, 113–114
  forensic, 114–115
executions
  attitudes toward, 34–35

and last requests, 48
delays of, 63–64, 73, 121–122
doctors at, 43–44
and geographical factor, 103–106, **105**
of innocent persons, 121–122
media coverage of, 50–52, **51**
and enforcement, 67–68
public, 48–50, 62–63
and race, 98–100, **66**
statistics, 21, 41, 54, 59, **66**, 67, 68–69, 73, 98, 99, 100, 104, **105**
types of, 35–44, **36**
witnesses to, 50
eyewitnesses, 113–114

false confessions, 113, 118–119
firing squads, 37–38
Ford v. *Wainright*, 17
forensic evidence, 114–115
Furman v. *Georgia*, 55–57, 67, 74, 80

Gacy, John Wayne, 73
gas chamber, 41–42
genetics, 19–20
Gideon v. *Wainwright*, 28, 109
Gilmore, Gary, 38
Glendening, Parris, 58, 119
governors, 33, 48, 57–59, 67–68, 117–119
Greece (ancient), 11–12
Gregg v. *Georgia*, 57

hanging, 35–37, **36**, 50
Hanssen, Robert, 14
Harris County, 104–106
hate crimes, 86
human rights, 35, 43, 55, 79–80, 84, 123–124
human nature, 70–71, 87–88

Illinois, 57–58, 117–119
incompetent counsel, 112–113

indictment, 25
Innocence Projects, 116–117
Innocence Protection Act, 119–120
innocent persons. *See* wrongful
  convictions
insanity pleas, 16–18

Jackson, Jesse Sr., 61–62
justice, **24**, 25–26, 73, 82–83
justice system
  appeals phase, 32–33
  clemency, 33
  defense attorneys, 28–29
  flaws, 111–115. *See also* wrongful
    convictions; sentencing
  judges' role, 31–32
  juries, 29–30
  penalty phases, 30–31, 56
  prosecution, 26–28
  trial phases, 30–31
juveniles, 22–23

Kemmler, William, 38
kidnapping, 13
Krone, Ray, 115–116, 117

last meal, 48
last words, 47, 49
Latin America, 10
lawyers
  defense, 28–29, 101–103, 112–113
  prosecution, 26–28, 106
legislation
  and DNA testing, 117, 119–120
  and insanity defense, 16–17
  and prisoners' rights, 119–120
  and sentencing bias, 96
  and terrorism, 16, 32
    See also states
Lennon, John, 18
Leopold, Nathan, **90**, 90–91
lethal injection, 42–46, **45**

life without parole (LWOP), 64–65,
  67, 72–73, 83, 90–91, 92–93
lynchings, 53–54, 95–96

Mailer, Norman, 92
Marshall, Thurgood, 74, 80, **81**, 121
Maryland, 58, 119
mass murder, 16
McVeigh, Timothy, **6**, 7–8, **15**, 52,
  71, 76–77, 85
mens rea, 27–28
mental retardation, 19, 113
Middle Ages, 12
Miller-El, Thomas, 30
mitigating factors, 27, 32, 56
Mobley, Stephen, 20
moral issues
  opposition views, 79–80, 83, 84–86
  support views, 77–79, 82–83, 84–85
murderers
  as authors, 91, 92
  family of, 85
  juvenile, 23
  and race, **97**, 98–100
  repeat offenders, 64–65, 92
  women as, 21–22

newspapers, 50–52, **51**, 83, 117–118
New Zealand, 10

objectivity, 25–26, 95
O'Connor, Sandra Day, 120
Oklahoma City bombing, **6**, 7–8, **15**
  See also McVeigh, Timothy
opposition
  activism, 8, **63**, 74, 91, **94**, 109
  deterrence, 70–75, **74**
  DNA testing, 117, 120
  Eighth Amendment, 54–57
  geographical factor, 104–106
  innocent persons, 120–121
  moral issues, 79–80, 83, 84, 85–86

moratoria, 57–59, 117–119
international, 123–124
poverty factor, 29, 102–103
race factor, 98–99, 103
rehabilitation, 90–92
televised executions, 52
trends, 53–54
Web sites, 137–138

parole, 57, 64–67, 72–73
penalty phases, 30–31, 56
penitentiaries, 44, 88–89, 92–93
See also prisons
plea bargaining, 26, 113
politics, 31, 122
polls, 57, 67, 77, 122, 124
poverty, 29, 101–103
Prejean, Sister Helen, 52, 102, 136
prisons, 44, 46, 48
See also penitentiaries
Prohibition, 54
prosecution, 26–27, 106
public defenders, 28–29, 101–103,
112–113
public opinion, 60–62, 67, 122, 124
See also opposition; support

rape, 13, 96, 109, 116
Reagan, Ronald, 88–93
Regan, Brian P., 14
rehabilitation, 88–93
Reno, Janet, 74
repeat offenders, 64–65, 92, 101
responsibility, 16–20, 22-23, 84
retribution
opposition views, 76–77, 79–80,
83, 84, 85–86
support views, 76, 77–79, 82–83,
84, 85
revenge, 76–77
right-to-life, 83
Ring v. *Arizona*, 31–32
Romans (ancient), 78
Rosenberg, Julius and Ethel, 13

Royko, Mike, 83
Rush, Benjamin, 79, 88
Ryan, George, 57–58, 117–119

Salem witch trials, 12
Scalia, Antonin, 84
Scottsboro Boys, 109, **109**
sentencing
and geography, 103–106, **105**
and guidelines, 26–28, 96,
103–106, **105**
and judges, 31–32
and the poor, 101–103
and race, **94**, 95–96, 98–101, **100**
statistics, 21, 30, **58**, 67–69, 98, **100**
serial killers, 16, 17
Shepard, Matthew, 86
Snyder, Ruth, 50–51, **51**
spies, 13–14
Stanford v. *Kentucky*, 22
states
and clemency, 33, 118–119
allowing death penalty, 14, 53–54,
55–57
and execution
disparities, 103–106
of juveniles, 22–23
methods, **45**
statistics, **105**
public, 49–50
insanity plea, 17
life without parole, 72
moratoria, 57–58, 117–119
public defenders, 28–29, 101–103
southern, 96, 104, 108–110
See also Illinois; legislation; Texas
support
activism, **6**, 8, **63**
deterrence, 62–65, 67–69
DNA testing, 121–122
geographical factor, 106
innocent prisoners, 121–122
moral issues, 77–79, 82-83, 84, 85
poverty factor, 103

prison life, 46
race factor, 99–101
rehabilitation, 92–93
trends, 54, 56–57
Web site, 137
Supreme Court
on the Eighth Amendment, 54–57,
80, 84
on executing the insane, 17
on executing mentally retarded
persons, 19
on judges, 31–32
on juries, 30, 108
on juveniles, 22–23
on kidnapping, 13
on race, 30, 108
on rape, 13
on poor defendants, 28, 102

Taylor, John Albert, 38
teenagers, 22–23
television, 52
terrorism, 16
Texas, 104–106
Thompson v. *Oklahoma*, 22
torture, 108, 118–119
treason, 12, 13–14
Turgenev, Ivan, 34
Twain, Mark, 50

United States
death penalty nation, 10, 123–124
early twentieth century, 41, 53–54,
79
eighteenth century, 12–13, 49, 62–
63, 79, 87-89
execution statistics, 21, 41, 54, **59**,
66, 67, 68–69, 73, 96, 98, 99,
100, 104, **105**
nineteenth century, 38, 49–50, 89
sentencing statistics, 21, 30, **58**,
67–69, 98, **100**
seventeenth century, 12–13, 20,
35, 48–49

treason, 12, 13–14
See also African Americans; executions; legislation; sentencing;
states; Supreme Court; wrongful convictions

victims
families of, 85–86
race of, **66**, **97**, 98, 101
rights of, 64–65, 83
vigilantes, 53–54, 76

Web sites, 137–138
Weems v. *U.S.*, 54
Westinghouse, George, 39
White, Byron, 67
Will, George, 62
witchcraft, 12
witnesses, 113–114
women, 13, 20–22, **66**
wrongful convictions
Baldwin, Brian, 108, 110, 114–115
causes, 111–115
Cruz, Rolando, 110–111
Illinois, 118–119
Krone, Ray, 115–116, 117
Leahy, Patrick, 119–120
opposition views, 120–121
Scottsboro boys, 109
support views, 121–122
Townsend, Jerry Frank, 113

Yates, Andrea, 21–22

About the Author

Ron Fridell has written for radio, TV, newspapers, and textbooks. He has written books on social and political issues, such as terrorism and espionage, and scientific topics, such as DNA fingerprinting and global warming. He taught English as a second language while a member of the Peace Corps in Bangkok, Thailand. He lives in Evanston, Illinois, with his wife Patricia and his dog, an Australian shepherd named Madeline.